living
coastal

inspirations for entertaining, decorating
and cooking california style

jolee pink

photographs by mike pawlenty

Copyright © 2013 Chefs Press, Inc.

Published by Chefs Press, San Diego, California
chefspress.com

President and Publisher: Amy Stirnkorb
CEO and Director of Photography: Mike Pawlenty

Text copyright © 2013 Jolee Pink
Photographs copyright © 2013 Mike Pawlenty / Chefs Press
Editor: Nancy Martin
Chef Paul Arias photo copyright © Eric Wolfinger / courtesy The Fishery
Chef Ricardo Heredia photo copyright © Marisa Holmes / courtesy Alchemy Restaurant
Chef Tim Johnson photo copyright © Jon Foster / courtesy Zenbu
Jolee Pink ceramics photos copyright © Jolee Pink
Artist James Stone photo copyright © Erik Christiansen / courtesy James Stone
Surfing Madonna photo copyright © Mark Patterson

The Publisher would like to give special thanks to the La Jolla Beach & Tennis Club for allowing us to photograph on their beautiful property for the cover and pages 52-53 and 64-65; and to all of the homeowners, businesses, restaurants, and chefs who generously gave of their time to our project, including:
The Allens, pages 40-41
The Arthurs, pages 10-11
The Gafners, pages 22-23
The Halls, pages 16-17 and 58-59
The Martin-Brehms, pages 34-35
The Martin-Shreiners, pages 70-71 and 100-101
One19 Living Studio, pages 28-29 and 46-47

ISBN: 978-0-9816222-8-6

First Edition
Printed in China

To Larry,

The Love of My Life

contents

foreword

SERGE DEDINA, WiLDCOAST EXECUTIVE DIRECTOR

On a sunny afternoon in February, I donned my wetsuit, grabbed my big-wave surfboard and made the trek to the mouth of the Tijuana River in Imperial Beach. As I walked down the beach toward the border with Mexico, I watched waves breaking more than a half mile offshore on the cobblestone reefs of the Sloughs, a popular surf spot and one of California's newest marine protected areas.

After making the long paddle to the lineup, I zeroed in on the double overhead waves breaking on the reef and the wildlife that surrounded me. A flock of brown pelicans bobbed along with the swells. Cormorants darted above me. Royal terns flew overhead. And a pod of bottlenose dolphins surfed large-set waves in between forays underwater for fish.

My paddle out at the Sloughs wasn't memorable for the half dozen waves I rode, but the feeling I had that day was. I felt I was part of something miraculous — waves traveling thousands of miles to break on the reef surfed by dolphins in a symmetry of perfection.

It's not surprising that I found abundant ocean wildlife in what is supposed to be the most polluted corner of California. The ocean here teems with life. Our kelp forests resemble marine rainforests. Docile leopard sharks fill up the underwater spaces of La Jolla Shores during the summer. Juvenile white sharks, born at the northern end of San Diego County, glide past thousands of surfers, divers, paddlers and swimmers on their way to hunt the elephant seals of Guadalupe Island, located south of Ensenada off the west coast of Baja California, Mexico. Blue whales, leviathans of the deep, move

quickly northward in the spring after spending the winter in the Gulf of California. Gray whales, our mascots of the sea, navigate our coastal waters by the thousands during their winter migration to Baja's empty desert lagoons.

We are lucky to live in what ocean photographer and author Glenn Vanstrum calls our "saltwater wilderness." Our coastline is the gateway to the vast aquatic region that covers much of our planet. It's an endless azure natural aquarium filled with wonder, life, mystery and joy.

I spend most of my free time in the ocean; so I see the world in a palette of aqua blues and greens. I crave the wetness and taste of saltwater, the churn and roar of waves. I am truly happy only when I am unbounded by the freedom of the open ocean.

But the ocean is bound by the impact of humans. We dispense huge amounts of pollutants, plastic and sediment into the sea every day. Our oceans are becoming more acidic, creating giant algae blooms and turning portions of the ocean into death zones. Fishermen travel farther and farther in search of fish to feed our endless appetites for seafood. In the great Pacific gyre (a circular current in the middle of the Pacific Ocean), ocean conservationist Charles Moore, an old friend, classic California surfer and waterman, discovered and reported on a sea of plastic and debris that is literally choking the ocean to death.

"There is more plastic than plankton out there," Moore said one day as he showed me a jar filled with a sample of seawater from one of his explorations aboard his research vessel, *The Algalita*. Moore, however, didn't stop with just talking about the plastic plague. He started a movement that works with government agencies and inspiring organizations such as the Surfrider Foundation to launch its Rise Against Plastics program.

In my own ocean conservation work with WiLDCOAST, the organization I co-founded and now run, we have engaged thousands of volunteers to clean up tons of ocean-bound plastic and Styrofoam in the Tijuana River Valley. My colleague, Paloma Aguirre, who has worked tirelessly on both sides of the U.S.-Mexico border to scour canyons and gullies for garbage, estimates that more than ten million Styrofoam cups are still buried in the Tijuana River.

There are remedies to our ocean crises. *Sustainability* is now a buzzword and a real solution. Many examples of ocean conservation success can already be found worldwide. In Cabo Pulmo National Park along Baja's East Cape, marine biologists worked with local fishing families and the Mexican government to create a marine park to protect the northernmost coral reef in North America. Together, they planned a carefully monitored "no-take zone" in the waters surrounding the reef, an area of more than 17,000 acres. Ten years later, researchers from La Jolla's Scripps Institution of Oceanography reported that fish biomass had increased 460 percent and called Cabo Pulmo one of the world's most "robust" marine reserves.

Further north along Baja's central Pacific Coast, fishermen in the village of Punta Abreojos have been fishing lobster and abalone sustainably for close to 60 years. Their fishing practices are so commendable that their lobster harvest received the Marine Stewardship Council (MSC) certification — the first community-based fishery in Latin America to receive such a commendation.

The recovery of our fish species and underwater ecosystems was the rationale behind the decision to create California's new system of marine-protected areas (MPAs). These underwater parks are designed to preserve some of our most iconic and precious marine ecosystems: the reefs and embayments where fish breed and hatch. Such protected habitats provide a place where fragile species can rest, recover and return in greater numbers.

The good news about MPAs is that we have time to help the ocean and its inhabitants recover their numbers. This planned recovery will help our seafood populations and allow fishermen the chance to make a better living in the future. We now know that the key to sustainable seafood is a partnership between conservationists, fishermen, chefs and restaurants to determine what species can be harvested sustainably and then promote those species to the consumer.

Despite the threats to the ocean, I am not going to stop eating seafood. I will continue to work to conserve the species and ecosystems, but I will also work with chefs and fishermen to promote sustainable harvesting. That is why the celebration of our coast and oceans in *Living Coastal* is so important. Food and art help us commemorate happy memories of wonderful meals on the seashore.

I am inspired by Jolee's homage to a place and state of mind that takes us to our last real oasis. After all, there is no better way to honor the sea's bounty than by eating a fresh plate of tasty seafood with friends and family while we watch the waves and wildlife that give us so much joy.

SERGE DEDINA is executive director of WiLDCOAST and author of *Saving the Gray Whale* and *Wild Sea: Eco-Wars and Surf Stories from the Coast of the Californias*. He has received the California Coastal Commission's "Coastal Hero Award" and the San Diego Zoological Society's Conservation Medal for his efforts to preserve the coast and ocean. He grew up and still lives and surfs in Imperial Beach.

introduction

What happens when top San Diego area chefs and artists connect to create consummate seaside delights? Meals turn into maritime magic! Each fun-filled chapter in *Living Coastal* features a different ocean-inspired theme for entertaining both indoors and out. This unique mix of tantalizing seafood recipes, extraordinary artistic creations, my company Wabisabi Green's modern eco table linens and clever decorating tips will inspire your next celebration.

Our acclaimed chefs spearhead the nutritious trend towards using fresh local produce and sustainable seafood. Since the region's long growing season supports plentiful small farms as well as farmers markets, and thriving local fisheries bring the bounty of the ocean to restaurant tables, these enterprising chefs take advantage of the readily available resources to dream up diversified market-driven menus.

The recipes in this book provide an exciting chance to learn from the experts — inventive cooks who use natural ingredients to prepare scrumptious seafood dishes. Since these chefs are well-traveled, their dishes reflect the international influences of numerous world cuisines including Italian, French, Mexican, Japanese and Thai.

Simplicity is key for plating style, and the chefs apply fine-art principles of color, shape and texture to design their presentations. Their visual creativity with tastes and composition will encourage you to bring your own personal style into play.

The artists involved in this project provide another compelling source of inspiration. The influence of the Pacific Ocean environment permeates their choice of relaxing beach colors and vivacious aquatic imagery. Using a wide spectrum of mediums such as ceramic, glass, metal, paints and succulents, these artists, including myself, add dimension and heart to the dining scene. The settings are meant to prompt you to look at your own environment for artistic inspiration. Sometimes unusual seashells, stones, colorful produce or foliage from your garden can achieve breathtaking tablescapes. The options are limitless!

Cooking and art are all about passion. Both elevate the senses, bring beauty and joy into our lives and connect us through cross-cultural experiences. The benefit of sourcing locally improves the wholesomeness of our food, the health of our environment and the community at large. We hope you enjoy reproducing these delicious dishes and use this book to unleash your own creativity, follow your culinary-artistic muse and savor many special memories with family and friends.

—Jolee Pink
Encinitas, CA

retro new year's eve

Mid-century modern evokes a happy retro-chic vibe and a welcomed sense of nostalgia. Popularized by the iconic television show *Mad Men*, think classic cocktails, Cadillacs, cat eyes and pencil ties! This design style, simple and clean, combines upbeat fun colors such as pink, turquoise and orange. No wonder it's a growing trend and perfect choice for a New Year's Eve celebration. Starlite Chef Kathleen Wise believes that the ideal meal to start the year comes directly from the sea. "What could be better than champagne with oysters? Or should I say, oysters with champagne? Either way, the simpler the better: served cold on the half-shell with Meyer lemon mignonette or served hot with Pernod, spinach and bread crumbs." Britt Neubacher's refined succulent table centerpiece and Wabisabi Green's retro-inspired Blue Fish table linens complete the scene with style and flair.

baked oysters
with pernod and spinach

serves 2

4 tablespoons butter
2 cloves garlic, chopped
2 pounds spinach, washed
2 ounces Pernod
Sea salt and freshly ground black pepper, to taste
½ cup bread crumbs
1 dozen oysters, shucked

MELT 1 tablespoon of butter in a medium pan and sauté garlic and spinach until wilted. Add Pernod and cook until the liquid has evaporated. Season with sea salt and black pepper. Melt remaining butter and mix with bread crumbs, seasoning them as well.
PREHEAT oven broiler.
ARRANGE oysters in an ovenproof dish. Top each one with spinach and then bread crumbs. Place on the middle rack of a broiler until bread crumbs are golden brown. Enjoy!

oysters
with meyer lemon mignonette

serves 2

3 Meyer lemons
1 shallot
Sea salt and freshly ground black pepper, to taste
1 dozen oysters, shucked

JUICE the lemons, finely chop the shallot, combine, and season with salt and pepper. Chill for at least an hour before serving with the oysters.

kathleen wise, starlite

The fundamental commitment to cooking and meal planning of Kathleen's German grandmother Verona and her great-aunt Adeline inspired Kathleen to become the food lover she is today. "Food holds so much memory," Kathleen says. "Emotions can be brought back in an instant by a whiff of a grilled hamburger, a taste of pumpkin pie or the thought of visiting your favorite restaurant again." She also believes in natural, local, sustainably-sourced food. "If we care about ourselves, our community and the little bit of world that we live in and call home, we also need to care about where our food comes from and how it's cultivated. If we continue to use the current model of unsustainable agricultural practices, we will not survive."

artist profile
britton neubacher, tend

San Diego is on the cutting edge of succulent design, and Britt Neubacher is at the forefront of the scene. Drawing materials and inspiration from the San Diego coastline, this featured centerpiece is an exploration of the fascinating place where the desert meets the ocean. "These soft coastal colors and highly textured succulents remind me of our regional tide pools so alive with repetitive patterns and sacred geometries," she explains. Intrigued by visual mimicry in nature, Britt admires how succulents can resemble ocean floor creatures. She believes that "simple is beautiful." Her design ethos is to "strip away until the piece's purest essence is revealed." Britt feels that living centerpieces like this ground us and bring beautiful, natural energy to the dining ritual by connecting us back to where we came from — and to each other.

it's game day

Make room on the couch and turn your home into game central! It's time to gather 'round and revel in the excitement of the big day. Beguile your buddies with a super spread of feisty finger foods and ice-cold brews. For a surefire touchdown, rustle up some Stone IPA Marinated Mahi-Mahi Skewers from URBN Chef Alex Carballo. Pair with Stone Cali-Belgique IPA for some game time fun. Elon Ebank's engaging *Hungry Fish* sculpture adds an artsy touch to the setting, and our lively School of Fish napkins are sure to score coastal points.

stone ipa marinated mahi-mahi skewers

with pineapple chimichurri

serves 4 (2 skewers per person)

MAHI-MAHI SKEWERS
1 pound mahi-mahi, sliced into 8 (3-inch) pieces
$1/2$ cup Stone IPA
1 tablespoon chili powder
Salt and freshly ground black pepper, to taste

CHIMICHURRI
1 tablespoon garlic, minced
2 tablespoons red onion, minced
$1/2$ bunch cilantro, minced
$1/4$ cup lemon juice
$1/2$ jalapeño, seeded and finely minced
$1/2$ cup pineapple, minced (fresh or canned)
Salt and freshly ground black pepper, to taste

FINISHING TOUCH
Shredded cabbage

MARINATE fish pieces in beer in a small shallow pan for about 20 minutes. Drain the excess liquid, sprinkle fish with chili powder, and season with salt and pepper. Skewer marinated mahi-mahi and set aside for grilling.
MIX garlic, onion, and cilantro in a bowl. Gently stir in lemon juice, jalapeño, and pineapple. Season with salt and pepper. Set chimichurri aside until ready to serve.
PREHEAT a grill to high.
GRILL mahi-mahi skewers for a few minutes, just long enough to mark them.
PILE cabbage on a plate and place fish skewers in a circle on top. Garnish with chimichurri, as desired. These skewers are great as a tray-passed appetizer or for a buffet table.

alex carballo, urbn coal fired pizza

Home-cooked meals colored Alex Carballo's childhood and sparked his passion for great food. "I love to have people over to my house and cook for them," Alex says. "In fact, this is also the reason I decided to make cooking my career. I have been very lucky to live and cook in San Diego, where we have local products that make cooking fun." In his past position at Stone Brewing World Bistro & Gardens, he embraced the restaurant's commitment to serving locally grown, small-farm ingredients. To maximize its environmental responsibility, Stone bought a 19-acre organic farm, giving Alex a unique opportunity to "play with different produce varieties" that he otherwise couldn't find. "I feel better knowing I have made a real effort to support a cause larger than myself and realize I make a difference even though I am only one person!"

stone farms

Stone Farms is a biodynamic small-scale grower supplying organic, sustainable produce to both the company's farm-to-table bistros. Farm Supervisor David Solomon views small farms as the "roots of our communities." He follows the practice of feeding the soil naturally with worms and decomposition. "All the essential nutrients needed for a plant to grow strong and healthy are the same as for the human body," David says.

elon ebanks

Elon grew up on the small, rugged island of Cayman Brac in the Caribbean. His family lived off the land, where they grew or caught their own food and raised chickens. "I lived on the beach, which was my playground," Elon recalls. "There was a bright orange coral reef underwater where I fished for mangrove snappers, big eye squirrelfish and lobsters. I was in the water every day and collected many dinners from the sea." Elon also loved to swim, skin dive, body surf and sail. Since he frolicked in warm tropical waters as a child, it's no wonder that Elon is drawn to portraying sea life. "When I started doing art, the first piece I made was a fish. That inspired me so much that I just kept making fish after fish."

movies & munchies

Inviting friends over to watch a movie is an ideal excuse for a casual get-together. Whether you're screening a classic or a comedy, roll out the red carpet, stock the snack bar and dim the lights! Freshly popped popcorn is a movie night must. But what else will make your guests feel like A-listers? Sea Salt Candy Company's toffees and caramels are melt-in-your-mouth bliss. And yummy Larb Goong/Thai Shrimp Wraps from Alchemy Chef Ricardo Heredia have definite star appeal. "This is a perfect appetizer," chef Ricardo says. "The flavors speak of the wonderful freshness of its ingredients, and the complexity of the combination hits all the notes on your palate." Whimsy and color infuse James Stone's glass sculpture. And our *Shark Attack Platter* and Rock Shrimp napkins play a starring role.

larb goong

thai shrimp wraps with red curry paste

makes 8

Chef's Notes: Ingredients can be found at your local farmers and Asian markets. You can also buy prepared red curry paste to save time.

RED CURRY PASTE
3 dried whole red chiles, lightly
   toasted and seeds removed
   (I prefer New Mexico or guajillo
   chiles)
1 tablespoon salt
1 stalk lemongrass, hard outer
   leaves removed, sliced small
1½ tablespoons galangal or ginger,
   sliced small
1 tablespoon coriander roots
   (commonly used in Thai cooking)
   or cilantro stems, sliced small
1 tablespoon kaffir lime zest
¼ cup garlic
¾ cup white onion, diced
1 teaspoon shrimp paste

2 tablespoons palm sugar
¼ cup coconut milk
¼ cup fish sauce
2 kaffir limes, juiced

SHRIMP
1 pound local shrimp or spot prawns,
   peeled and deveined
1 bunch cilantro leaves, chopped
   (or micro cilantro)

FINISHING TOUCHES
1 head bibb lettuce leaves
½ red onion, sliced
1 bunch mint leaves (or micro mint)
Fresh lime wedges
1 cup peanuts, chopped

BEGIN the red curry paste by processing the dried chiles and salt into a powder in a food processor with the blade attachment. Add lemongrass and galangal and process into rough fibers. Add coriander roots or cilantro, lime zest, and garlic, pulsing after adding each ingredient. Add onion and shrimp paste.
FINISH the red curry paste by combining 1 tablespoon of the curry mixture, palm sugar, coconut milk, fish sauce, and lime juice in a food processor until fully incorporated. Reserve remaining curry mixture for another use.
BRING a stockpot full of water to a boil. Cook shrimp for 90 seconds. Transfer to an ice bath. Once cool, dry on paper towels, and chop into large pieces. Toss in the curry paste, add cilantro leaves and let marinate for a minimum of 1 hour.
PORTION shrimp into lettuce cups and top with onion, mint, a squeeze of lime, and chopped nuts.

ricardo heredia, alchemy

Like most chefs, Ricardo became interested in cooking at an early age. He credits his grandmother's influence as his main reason for entering the culinary world. "Combinations of sounds, smells and flavors left a deep impression in my childhood and led to an inquisitive exploration of foods," Ricardo explains. "From hanging out at our Vietnamese neighbors for food at age eight to roasting my first chicken at age nine, part of that childlike curiosity is still embedded in what I do every day. Cooking requires an infinite amount of knowledge and fuels my constant quest to learn and, more importantly, teach my craft to others." As a chef, father and teacher, Ricardo strongly believes in adopting practices that will change the future: "Farmers are very giving people. Their hours are long. The pay is not going to make them financially rich, but they are devoted to producing the wonders of nature for people to enjoy. Sourcing local produce and supporting responsible fishery-and-animal harvesting means I am teaching children the importance of sustaining our planet's resources and giving our customers the best possible products I can get."

sea salt
candy company

Partners Lisa and Gretchen Bender started
selling their line of toffees and salted caramels
at local farmers markets before branching out online,
opening their first retail shop and then expanding
nationwide. The toffee recipe came from Lisa's family line
of candy makers. Gretchen concocted the caramel recipe
to satisfy her father's sweet tooth when he lost his sense
of taste due to throat cancer. Together, they believe in using
simple, premium-quality, all-natural ingredients in their confections:
almonds from Chico, unrefined rock sea salt from Sonoma and
gourmet chocolate from San Francisco. "We don't skimp," Gretchen
explains. "Everything is done by hand, one batch at a time. It's hand-
stirred and hand-poured." And the combination of wholesome ingredients,
hand-crafted care and love makes the candy a savory-sweet delight.

At his environmentally conscious studio, James Stone creates sea creatures and marine-themed sculptures that portray the beauty of the ocean's diverse flora and fauna. In his latest mega-work, *Last Call Before We Eat Them All*, James addresses the delicate balance of our world's largest ecosystem and its inhabitants. His message of eco-awareness leaps from the 30-foot wall on which he works. This dazzling and powerful oeuvre serves as a warning that fish and other sea life are disappearing at historically unprecedented rates due to overfishing and overconsumption.

While James hopes his work creates a dialogue, he meditates on the process. "True creativity must start with the pure and raw feeling in one's heart," he explains. "Creativity is born in that space where there are no pictures, no words — just a strong emotional feeling devoid of form or function. It is from the heart that the emotional responses move into the head where they begin to take shape in the form of ideas." Interestingly, James approaches the dining experience from a theatrical perspective: "When preparing for a party or a simple dinner with friends, I like to think of these moments in our lives as a stage play. In each dinner, there is a storyline complete with a plot, main characters, minor roles, sets, lights, music and props used to enhance the atmosphere and experience. Glass became my medium of choice because it makes a good material for props, and it also allows me to use magical light to affect my audience on a much deeper level — a force that motivates me to create art."

spring fling

Colorful blooms appear, weather warms and days grow longer as beach season grows nearer. Why not welcome this regeneration with a festive springtime feast? Bejewel a table generously with fresh flowers. For a seaside twist, opt for shades of spring using seafoam greens and aquas. Shown are Cheryl Tall's intricately textured ceramics, Tara Teipel's lovely floral design and our Coral napkins. Welcome spring with Local Pan-Seared Sardines from Sessions Public Chef Brandon Brooks. "When you bite into the sardine, it just screams *fish* in a good way," Brandon says. "It's everything you want to taste in the ocean: oily, salty and just really good for you." Sardines are not only a small and delicious choice for the plate, but they also contain high amounts of omega-3 fatty acids and almost no mercury due to their size and relatively short lives. A sustainable variety of fish, sardines are extremely easy to find up and down the West Coast.

pan-seared local sardines
with tapenade and coleslaw

serves 6

Chef's Notes: It's best to make the tapenade a day in advance. I recommend using either small San Marzano or Stupice (stu-peez) tomatoes, both of which are grown locally in San Diego.

TAPENADE
3 to 4 heirloom tomatoes (about
⅟₂ cup roasted)
2 to 3 red bell peppers (about
⅟₂ cup roasted)
⅛ cup capers
¼ cup red onion, finely diced
2 tablespoons honey
6 cloves roasted garlic, sautéed in olive oil
and minced
⅟₂ teaspoon salt, or to taste

DRESSING
⅟₂ cup orange juice
2 tablespoons rice wine vinegar
⅟₂ tablespoon salt

COLESLAW
1⅟₂ cups kale, roughly chopped
1⅟₂ cups mache (I prefer crown mache)
1 apple, cored and thinly sliced
⅟₂ cup fennel, thinly sliced (save tops
for optional garnish)

SARDINES
1⅟₂ pounds (12) whole fresh sardines,
scaled, cleaned, rinsed, patted dry
(2 sardines per person)
1 cup white flour
2 teaspoons salt
1 teaspoon white pepper
¼ cup olive oil

PREHEAT oven to 200°F.

PLACE the tomatoes and peppers in a shallow ovenproof baking dish and slowly roast for 6 to 8 hours, until they look dehydrated but are still soft to the touch. The skin should not be hard or crispy. Set aside to cool and finely dice.

MAKE the tapenade by combining the tomatoes and bell peppers with the remaining ingredients in a bowl. Cover with plastic wrap and let sit at room temperature overnight for the best flavor.

MIX all dressing ingredients in a bowl and set aside.

TOSS all coleslaw ingredients in a bowl. Add dressing just before serving.

PREPARE the sardines by combining flour, salt, and white pepper in a bowl. Dredge sardines in the mixture, making sure to coat each piece thoroughly. Drizzle olive oil evenly onto the surface of a large hot skillet, and place sardines one at a time into skillet. Don't overcrowd. Cook for 1⅟₂ minutes per side, or until light golden brown. Drain on paper towels before serving.

TOSS the coleslaw and dressing. Portion the sardines among 6 plates. Garnish with tapenade and fennel tops, if desired.

brandon brooks, sessions public

Brandon grew up in a family that didn't always have the time or money to eat properly. "My mom raised me by herself and worked hard to put what food she could afford on the table," he recalls. "But watching my grandmother and great grandmother cook as a youngster motivated me to eat better as an adult." Working in the sport fishing industry, Brandon eventually took a job as a cook in a small galley. Today, he is passionate about local seafood. "Because our fishing boats don't have to travel far to access both Mexican and Central California waters, we enjoy warm and cold water species at different times of the year," he explains. Brandon also appreciates the region's long growing season: "The best thing about being a chef in San Diego is the amount of food you can work with that's available at our fingertips. It's exciting because there's always something new that's hitting the market. You can really change your menu on a regular basis and always have fresh flavors."

smoke & mirrors cocktail company

Formerly heralded as one of Boston's most beloved bartenders, Chris Simmons (shown right) worked with some of the best chefs in Bean Town. "This was instrumental in helping me understand the importance of fresh ingredients and how to successfully incorporate them into cocktails in a way that is approachable, fun and creative." He now manages The Pony Room in Rancho Santa Fe, where he proudly carries more than 100 tequilas. Chris's equally experienced business partner, Shawn Barker, trained in Las Vegas under cocktail giants Francisco LaFranconi and Tony Abu-Ganim before designing bar menus for Bertrand at Mister A's and numerous Wolfgang Puck restaurants. Currently, he helms the program at The Patio in Pacific Beach. Together, the Smoke & Mirrors team avoids over-conceptualized concoctions in favor of straightforward but inventive drinks. They love to incorporate locally sourced produce from places such as Chino Farms. When developing a cocktail recipe, Chris and Shawn start with a spirit; then they imagine taste profiles: fruit-based, sweet, tart or herbal. From there, it's an enjoyable yet endless process of experimentation.

smiles in the morning cocktail

serves 1

4 ($^1/_2$-inch) slices cucumber
$^3/_4$ ounce St-Germain elderflower liqueur
2 ounces Hendrick's Gin
$^1/_2$ ounce freshly squeezed lime juice
$^1/_2$ ounce simple syrup

Edible flowers, garnish
Cucumber slice, garnish

MUDDLE cucumber and St-Germain in a shaker glass. Add remaining ingredients and fill with ice. Shake vigorously. Strain over fresh ice in a rocks glass. Garnish with edible flowers or cucumber slice. Cheers!

During a beach walk, Cheryl Tall collected a pocketful of shells to use as a reference while sculpting her *Seaform Collection*. She took a free-flowing design approach to emulate the movement of waves and used textured glazes to mimic sand. Then she added pulverized copper to infuse the pieces with watery aqua tints. In 2000, Cheryl lived in the coastal town of Stuart, Florida, where she recalls, "We often served seafood when we entertained on our boat or by the pool. I derived inspiration from my son, Nick Tall, who is now a chef in Hong Kong. Even as a young teenage cook, Nick lingered over plate choices for the seafood he was preparing, often choosing one of my handmade ceramic serving pieces. He taught me that appreciation of fine food rests not only in the taste buds but also in the eye. How a meal is presented adds immensely to its enjoyment."

tapas by the sea

Traditional Spanish small plates, prepared simply yet big on flavor, are called *tapas*. The concept originated from slices of bread or meat used as "covers" to keep flies out of glasses of sherry. Since these savory party snacks are casually shared, tapas and the Spanish spirit can turn a regular meal into a fun-filled evening full of laughter and lively conversation. Add an ocean view and a great bottle of red, such as Fallbrook Winery's estate grown 33° North BDX — and *la vida es muy buena*. For this table, The Fishery Chef Paul Arias prepared succulent Steamed Mussels and Northwest Crab Cakes. He used roasted chili butter to add scintillating spice and richness to the mussels, and he used shrimp as a binder in the crab cakes to create a unique and flavorful twist. Karen Athens' hand-painted runner and organic palm frond sculpture enhance Wabisabi Green's Sand Dollar napkins and bring the whole composition together.

mussels
with fennel and linguica in red jalapeño broth

serves 1

Chef's Notes: Recipe can easily be multiplied.

JALAPEÑO BUTTER
5 or 6 red jalapeños
1/2 cup (1 stick) butter, softened

MUSSELS
1 tablespoon shallots, minced
1 tablespoon garlic, minced
1 tablespoon fennel, minced
1 pound mussels, cleaned, debearded, and
    patted dry
1/2 cup white wine
1 cup fish stock
1 lemon, juiced
2 ounces linguica (Portuguese sausage), cooked
    and sliced
Salt and freshly ground black pepper, to taste

FINISHING TOUCHES
1/2 bunch fresh cilantro leaves, chopped
Olive oil, for drizzling
Good crusty bread, sliced and toasted

PREHEAT a grill to high.
ROAST jalapeños until skins blister. Cover and let cool.
Peel and deseed. In a food processor, purée butter and
chiles. Transfer to a small bowl and refrigerate.
SAUTÉ shallots, garlic, and fennel with 1 tablespoon
jalapeño butter in a hot skillet on medium-high heat
for 1 minute. Add mussels and sauté for 2 minutes,
stirring frequently. Add wine carefully to deglaze the
pan, then add fish stock. Cover tightly and steam for
3 to 4 minutes, or until all mussels open. Discard any

that don't. Add another tablespoon of jalapeño butter,
lemon juice, and linguica. Taste and season.
PLACE mussels in a wide-rimmed bowl, sprinkle with
lots of cilantro, drizzle with olive oil and serve with
pieces of crusty bread.

northwest crab cakes

serves 6

1 pound cooked Dungeness crab meat
2 ounces raw shrimp meat, puréed in food processer
$^1/_2$ cup mayonnaise
1 teaspoon Sambal chili sauce
1 teaspoon Dijon mustard
1 tablespoon fresh parsley, chopped
$^1/_4$ teaspoon Old Bay seasoning
2 tablespoons fresh lemon juice
$^1/_2$ cup panko bread crumbs
1 teaspoon sea salt
2 cups panko bread crumbs, for coating cakes
Olive oil, as needed for sautéing

GENTLY mix first 10 ingredients in a large bowl until well combined.
FORM into 1-ounce cakes (between 18 and 20).
COAT each cake in bread crumbs on both sides.
SAUTÉ the cakes, a few at a time, in olive oil on medium heat until golden brown on both sides.
SERVE each person 3 (1-ounce) crab cakes. They are delicious on their own, or with an optional light seasonal salad, such as shaved beets and tangerine tossed with frisée, lemon juice, and good olive oil.

paul arias, the fishery

When Paul Arias was thirteen, he worked in a restaurant that sold Belgian-style *frites*. "I was taught how to make mayonnaise from scratch and have been hooked ever since," he says. "Something so simple was very inspiring to me at that age." Jointly owned Pacific Shellfish Seafood Company next to The Fishery allows Paul to offer diners sustainable seafood served fresh off the boat. "The choice of seasonal produce and fish that comes in daily makes my job quite stimulating," he says. "We're all about wild fish. Working with well-managed fisheries ensures the future of seafood." Paul educates people to taste the difference between farmed and wild-caught fish. He also transforms traditionally meat-based preparations into interesting specialties that include sausage made from swordfish, bacon made from salmon and chorizo made from shrimp.

jayla siciliano, bon affair

Jayla Siciliano came up with the idea of Bon Affair because she wanted a healthy wine alternative to fit her active professional lifestyle. She worked with beverage experts to develop the first truly light, incredible tasting all-natural wine spritzer on the market. The product contains hydrating electrolytes with half the calories of regular wine. Jayla enthusiastically comments, "We don't put any compromising ingredients in Bon Affair (no preservatives, no sugars, zilch, zero, nada). When there are situations where regular wine is a bit too heavy, an option with less alcohol (and without the filling/bloating aspects of beer) makes us feel alive and good. You know the difference you feel when you eat heavy Italian food as opposed to when you eat sushi? We like to think of Bon Affair as the sushi of the wine world."

Sauvignon Blanc Tasting Note: Refreshing blend of real California wine with pure carbonated water creates bright citrus notes and a clean, crisp taste similar to champagne or Prosecco.

vin de fleurs cocktail
recipe by jeff josenhans, mixologist, grant grill

serves 1 (recipe can easily be multipled)

1 part St. George Terroir Gin (California-based, using Douglas fir, coastal sage, and bay laurel)
¼ part coconut water
1 part muscat grape syrup or clear agave nectar
5 or 6 dashes jasmine flower water (available at amazon.com)
5 parts Bon Affair sauvignon blanc
Jasmine flower, optional

SHAKE all ingredients except Bon Affair in a shaker and pour over ice in a large tumbler or larger wine glass. Add Bon Affair and stir. Garnish with jasmine flower, if desired.

Karen's time spent living in the Caribbean inspired her *Travel Destination* painting series. Created by richly layering color, the abstract works celebrate the islands and a deep connection to the ocean. "Walking endless hours on sandy beaches with waves crashing on the shore while listening to the whisper of windy palm trees allows me to look deep into my creative soul," Karen relects. Her aqua-hued runner and bronze-tinged frond sculpture bring the breathtaking beauty of nature to the table. She believes that art is key to any activity, especially the dining experience. "Color and design greatly affect our appetite and the way we feel. My work is intended to evoke the gentle sway of palm trees paired with the ebb and flow of the sea to create a relaxing coastal setting."

shower sweetness

What better way to make the bride or mother-to-be feel special than by throwing a lavish shower? Break out your best china and decorate with abandon. Here Tara Teipel showcases a set inherited from her grandfather. Using these exquisite pieces on special occasions, Tara believes, "really takes the dining experience to an elevated level — memorable in beauty, history and delicacy. In my opinion, it makes the food taste that much better. It's worth all the dusting off and polishing!" Tara's sumptuous centerpieces mixed with gemstones share the table with Wabisabi Green's Bloom table linens scattered with abalone shells. A bottle of Fallbrook Winery Chardonnay is the perfect companion for the flavorful snapper recipe created by Chandler's Chef Pascal Vignau.

local red snapper

with roasted sweet corn and cilantro vinaigrette

serves 1 (recipe can easily be multiplied)

Chef's Notes: When choosing fish, the chef advises, "Ask your fishmonger what's the freshest fish available that day. Make sure the fish is firm, bright in color and has no fishy odor."

2 ears yellow corn with husks
$1/2$ cup extra virgin olive oil, divided use
1 tablespoon fresh cilantro, chopped
1 lemon, juiced, divided use
Salt and freshly ground black pepper, to taste
6 ounces local red snapper, fileted and deboned, skin on one side
$1/4$ pound (4 ounces) asparagus
Salt and freshly ground black pepper, to taste
Grilled lemon, garnish
Endive, garnish

PREHEAT grill to high.
GRILL yellow corn for 6 to 10 minutes. Remove from grill and cool. Peel husks, slice the kernels from the cob, and place in a bowl. Mix with $1/4$ cup olive oil, chopped cilantro, fresh lemon juice, and season with salt and pepper. Set aside at room temperature.
PLACE remaining olive oil in a sauté pan and heat to medium. Place seasoned fish in pan flesh side down. Sear for 3 to 4 minutes (depending on size of fish) on each side.
GRILL asparagus until tender, and season with additional olive oil, salt, pepper, and lemon juice.
PLATE asparagus and corn and top with snapper filets. Garnish with grilled lemon and endive.

pascal vignau, chandler's

French born chef Pascal Vignau speaks with pride about the three generations of his family in the food business. At the age of ten, Pascal began helping his grandmother in the kitchen and developed a fascination for cooking. This childhood grounding catapulted his illustrious career when he moved from executive chef of the AAA Five-Diamond restaurant at the Four Seasons Aviara Resort in Carlsbad to owner/chef of the top-rated Savory Restaurant in Encinitas. "I love the passion and creativity that is generated from being a chef," Pascal says. "I love traveling to various countries and discovering new foods and new cultures." Now at Chandler's, the Hilton Carlsbad Oceanfront Resort eatery, Pascal specializes in simple, modern international and home-style cuisine. He starts with the freshest ingredients available, opting for locally grown whenever possible. The resulting dishes are not overly complicated, yet they remain big on flavor. The Local Red Snapper and Sweet Corn recipe is a good example. Pascal notes that red snapper is best during the summer complemented with seasonal vegetables.

fallbrook winery

From the top of Fallbrook Winery's highest vineyard, you can look out across miles of the region's green rolling hills all the way to the Pacific Ocean. That's partly what makes Fallbrook wines so great. Owner and founder Ira Gourvitz knew, from the very beginning, that this unique location — nearly 1,000 feet up in the Pala Mesa Mountains — contained the raw materials to make exceptional wine. The topography of this particular area creates microclimates that are ideal for growing wine grapes. Furthermore, the soil is mostly decomposed granite, and the ocean breezes keep the grapes happy even during the hottest summers. Although the building blocks of an exceptional vineyard were there from the beginning, it's still taken many years of hard work to establish Fallbrook Winery's reputation. Now Ira and the winery's talented team are finally enjoying the *fruits* of their labor. Fallbrook's estate-grown label, 33° North, has blossomed, and the wines have been recognized with awards and praise from many national and international competitions.

tara teipel, lemongrass

Tara Teipel's artwork brings a slice of nature indoors. She creates "living centerpieces that incorporate plant materials such as succulents, mosses and tillandsias infused with gemstones and crystals." Tara loves how the succulents resemble the textures and shapes of life under the sea. The precious minerals she uses remind her of the sparkle that hits the ocean from the reflection of the sun. "My hope is that these centerpieces remind people to tap into the balance and joy that the ocean provides on a daily basis." Working out of her garden studio, Tara hears the sounds of nature as her backdrop. She views the process of creating as both visual and visceral. Once Tara sees a concept actualize in her mind's eye, she collects materials and completes her pieces in a near meditative state of rapture. "The spectacularly beautiful results can magnify the enjoyment of a fine meal," Tara says. "I feel the living centerpieces set the mood and create an experience that not only grounds us, but at the same time, uplifts our spirits."

trip to the tropics

Imagine balmy breezes, coconut-pineapple-plumeria-scented air and lush oceanic vistas. Bring the tropics home by hosting your very own island pool party. Provide your guests with plenty of resort-style amenities: comfy lounge furniture, munchies, drinks, tunes, sunscreen and sensuous seafood. Then dive in! Interior designer Kim Nadel's glamorous backyard in sunny lime, tangerine and turquoise provides a dazzling setting for our spread. Chef Andrew Spurgin whipped up crowd-pleasing Salt-Baked Spot Prawns. "When I entertain at home, I want to sit and enjoy the time at the table with my guests," Andrew says. "This dish allows me that pleasure, and I also enjoy the family-style interactive approach. Plus it has a dramatic presentation and is just a breeze to prepare!" The prawns are served with effervescent white sangria using Bon Affair Sauvignon Blanc Wine Spritzer served on my vivid ceramic *Starfish Tray*. My Tropical Frond napkins, jewel-toned Dahlia pillows and Niche's SHAPE Series bench complete the picture.

salt-baked spot prawns
with aromatics, lemon and black mayonnaise

serves 6

Chef's Notes: If you can't get live spot prawns, use 18 whole (U10) shrimp in their shell.

BASIC MAYONNAISE
2 teaspoons sea salt (I prefer Maldon brand)
2 egg yolks (very fresh, organic is best)
1 egg
³/₄ tablespoon Dijon mustard
¹/₄ teaspoon granulated sugar
1 tablespoon rice wine vinegar
1 cup canola oil

LEMON MAYONNAISE
¹/₄ lemon, zested
¹/₂ tablespoon fresh lemon juice, or to taste

BLACK MAYONNAISE
¹/₂ tablespoon rice wine vinegar
Squid ink, as needed (available at amazon.com)

PRAWNS
2 (3-pound) boxes kosher salt
6 star anise pods
6 cinnamon sticks
2 tablespoons whole black peppercorns
18 whole live spot prawns (hold in ice water so they don't leap around)

FINISHING TOUCHES
Spot prawns often have roe. Simply remove and serve as a garnish, if desired

QUICKLY pulse salt, egg yolks, and egg in food processor until just blended. Add mustard, sugar, and rice wine vinegar. With the processor going, slowly add the oil in a very thin stream until the mixture thickens. You may not need to use all of the oil. If your mayonnaise becomes too thick, add a little water. Taste and adjust acid and salt. Keep refrigerated until ready to use. Use this basic mayonnaise recipe as a base for both the lemon and black mayonnaise.

FOLD in the zest and juice to one-half the basic mayonnaise recipe to make the lemon mayonnaise. Taste and adjust until satisfied with lemony flavor. Keep refrigerated until ready to serve.

FOLD in vinegar and squid ink to desired blackness to one-half the basic mayonnaise recipe to make the black mayonnaise. Keep refrigerated until ready to serve.

PREHEAT oven to 550°F.

PREPARE the prawns by spreading a 2-inch layer of salt into two heavy 11x14-inch roasting pans. Place remaining salt in a casserole dish.

PLACE the pans and casserole dish in the oven for 20 minutes. Remove the roasting pans from the oven, leaving the casserole dish in oven.

COMBINE star anise, cinnamon sticks, and peppercorns. Divide in half, reserving half. Using a wooden spoon, stir the first half of spice mix into the two roasting pans.

PLACE 9 prawns on the hot salt in each pan. Remove the casserole dish from oven and stir in remaining spice mix. Cover the prawns in both pans with about 2 more inches of this hot spiced salt.

LET the prawns sit covered on a heat-safe surface. Small to medium prawns should be cooked through in about 5 minutes. If the spot prawns are large, put the pans back in the oven for 3 more minutes.

CARRY the roasting pans to the table. Provide your guests with small metal tongs to remove prawns and small pastry brushes to dust off salt. New half-inch paint brushes also work well.

PEEL and eat! Garnish with roe, and serve with black and lemon mayonnaise, a big salad, and perhaps some asparagus. I love this dish for entertaining because it is so easy to make and participatory for your guests!

andrew spurgin, chef/event architect

Andrew's fascination with the food industry started with his childhood in London, where he grew up in his aunt's restaurant and his uncle's butcher shop. When edibles inform your childhood, you learn to appreciate their nuances at an early age. "I lived half a block from the Borough Market," Andrew recalls. "The rough-and-tumble Cockney 'Barrow Boys' there took me under their wing. As a child, I never wanted to be a cowboy or a fireman, just to be around anything food-related." Adhering to the philosophy that "the season drives the plate," Andrew follows sustainable practices to support the local economy and to provide both fresher and better products. "I think that sustainable food practices should be a natural fit for all regions, not just here in San Diego," Andrew says. "It's inspiring to see how many in our community are embracing that ethos. Just look at the number of farmers markets that avail themselves to us. I believe there are 60 here in our county. San Diego has more organic farms than any region in the U.S., and we grow a staggering 200 types of produce. In a word, we are blessed."

artist profile
jolee pink, wabisabi green

Since I grew up on the West Coast, I'm naturally drawn to the tranquility of the ocean. My coastal lifestyle inspires me to explore the world's sea life, a source of seemingly endless variety, color, form and texture. I start by sketching out ideas. Then comes the fun part of transforming a flat design and pile of mud into a three-dimensional sculpture that captures the essence of a living being. After firing, I meticulously apply multilayered glazes to achieve just the right radiant color combination to give the piece spirit. My ceramic sculpture and eco-friendly table linens bring art and color to the table. Also, the right environment enhances the enjoyment of any meal. What could be more central to the overall satisfaction of dining than the ambiance? Before we see the food, we feel the room, the setting, the sense of where we are. It's this blend of beauty and nature that encourages diners to share a unique experience: a meal where the usual becomes the extraordinary!

surfside serenity

A day at the beach brings vacation to mind. From wide sandy shores to rocky tidal pools, Southern California's extensive coastline and mild weather seduce us to play in the sun. Bring the surf to the seashore with an epicurean delight: Baja Lobster Roll Au Jus from MIHO Chef Rocio Siso-Gurriaran. "It's a fun recipe to prepare and eat," says chef Rocio. "For lobster lovers it's a must." Serve the delicious dish alongside our Lobster napkins, outdoor pillows and Grace Swanson's nautical gourds. Now you've got the makings for some beachside bliss!

baja lobster roll au jus

serves 4 to 6

MAYONNAISE
4 egg yolks
1 tablespoon Dijon mustard
2 tablespoons fresh lemon juice
Salt, to taste
2 cups blended oil (75% canola, 25% extra virgin olive)

LOBSTER SALAD
3 gallons water
3 teaspoons fresh parsley, chopped
1 bay leaf
3 teaspoons fresh chives, chopped

3 teaspoons fresh tarragon, chopped
4 (1¼-pound) Baja lobsters
2 tablespoons fennel, minced
2 tablespoons red onion, minced
2 tablespoons celery, diced
½ lemon, zested and juiced
Salt and freshly ground black pepper, to taste

AU JUS
4 tablespoons butter
4 lobster bodies, chopped into small pieces
3 cloves garlic, smashed
2 cups mirepoix (white onion, carrot, celery, and
    fennel), roughly chopped

1 tablespoon tarragon, chopped
1 tablespoon thyme leaves
1 tablespoon fennel fronds
Pinch anise seed
Pinch cayenne pepper
Pinch freshly ground black pepper
Pinch ground cloves
Pinch smoked paprika
Pinch curry powder
Pinch mustard seed
1 bay leaf
1 cup tomato, chopped
1 cup dry white wine
1 cup half & half or heavy cream
Salt and freshly ground black pepper, to taste

FINISHING TOUCHES
4 to 6 hot dog buns or lobster rolls, toasted
Shaved fennel and celery leaves

COMBINE yolks, mustard, lemon juice, and salt in
a bowl while whisking in oil in a slow steady stream.
Cover and refrigerate until needed.
BRING water to a boil in a large pot and add herbs.
Place lobsters in the water, cover, and turn off the heat.
Let sit for 10 minutes. Transfer lobsters to a sheet tray
to cool. Separate the tails from the bodies, saving all
the liquid that is released. Remove tail meat and discard
the vein. Chop lobster meat and combine in a bowl
with ½ cup mayonnaise, fennel, red onion, and celery,
finishing with zest and juice. Season with salt and
pepper, to taste. Cover and refrigerate until needed.
BROWN the butter in a saucepot, add chopped lobster
bodies and stir for 1 minute. Add garlic, mirepoix, and
remaining herbs and spices, and continue to sauté to
build a nutty and sweet flavor. Add tomatoes and wine.
Let alcohol cook off, and reduce until the ingredients
are almost dry. Add half & half or cream to the lobster
base, bring to a boil, stirring constantly and season with
salt and pepper, to taste.
FILL buns or rolls generously with chilled lobster salad,
garnish with fennel and celery leaves and serve with a
dish of hot lobster jus on the side.

rocio siso-gurriaran, miho gastrotruck

For Spanish-born, Michelin-star-restaurant-trained
Chef Rocio (pictured center), cooking and family
togetherness are interconnected. "I grew up in a
family where every meal was almost an event,"
Rocio recalls. "For lunch and dinner we stopped
whatever we were doing to sit around the table,
eat, talk and share. My passion for cooking comes
from my love of food and is a way for me to create
healthy relationships with others." As a pioneer of
the San Diego food truck scene, MIHO (founders
Kevin Ho, pictured above left, and Juan Miron)
helped popularize farm-to-street fare. Rocio's
enthusiasm for local seasonal cuisine supports
MIHO's dedication to thoughtful sourcing as a way
to bring sustainable and affordable food to the
community. When preparing her lobster roll dish,
Rocio suggests using fresh spiny Baja lobster and
serving the jus in a small container to prevent the
intense concentration of flavors from overpowering
the briny brilliance of the lobster salad.

Home to the award-winning Marine Room and one of California's few private beaches (shown in the previous spread), the treasured La Jolla Beach & Tennis Club offers the best in barefoot luxury. The breathtaking oceanfront resort blends old world charm with modern-day amenities and recreation. Guests are encouraged to enjoy the surf and turf without the crowds. Just offshore is the San Diego-La Jolla Underwater Park, a 6,000-acre marine life preserve that is popular with swimmers, snorkelers, scuba divers and kayakers. Located within the park is the Ecological Reserve, a no-fishing and no-scavenging safe haven for numerous species of oceanic flora and fauna, including spotted leopard sharks, sea lions, dolphins and migrating whales.

catalina offshore products

Catalina Offshore is a thriving company that specializes in local sustainable seafood from San Diego and the northern Baja area. Local species, such as California Gold sea urchin, California halibut and Baja red grouper, are just a few varieties of seafood that make up the daily bounty. Director of Marketing and Public Relations/Fishmonger extraordinaire Tommy Gomes explains, "We try to harvest healthy stock by using a non-destructive fishing practice with minimal damage to the habitat and minimal bycatch. Our sea urchin divers handpick each and every harvest. Most of our Baja Panga fisherman use hook-and-line hand lines which are much better at targeting fish than big nets dragging along the bottom causing damage to the ocean floor." Tommy's immense knowledge makes him so popular with local chefs that many have him on speed dial. "Trust your *true* fishmonger," Tommy says. "Ask questions. Know what part of the world your fish comes from."

artist profile grace swanson, gourds by grace

Grace Swanson, whose formative years were spent in Africa, fashions mini masterpieces out of gourds. Her appreciation for this ancient, organic art form coincides with her interest in early history — gourd crafting has been around for several thousand years. "I enjoy working with gourds because they come in such a variety of shapes and sizes," Grace says. "There are an infinite number of ways to transform each gourd into a unique creation." Grace lives near the water and uses colors and motifs of the sea in her work. "I incorporate the blues, aquas, turquoises and greens that remind me of the Pacific Ocean," she explains. "In fact, one piece is embellished with shells I picked up from a sandy beach." Since cultures around the world have used gourds to hold water, beer, milk, grain and more, Grace expects that her creations could be used as exotic dinnerware. "Imagine the shell-enhanced gourd as an unconventional but elaborately crafted artisan bowl for a crisp, fresh salad," she suggests. "Any of my gourds make unusual decorative centerpieces and conversation starters at the dining table. They are right at home in the dining room or kitchen. After all, they started out as fruits."

baja-style bash

Southern California cooking is strongly influenced by Mexican cuisine. Baja-style Mexican dishes emphasize fresh ingredients that often include seafood. The Crispy Whole Bass Tacos from Kelvin Chef Simon Dolinky are a fresh spin on San Diego's iconic fish tacos. Simon remembers, "On a family vacation to Mexico, my dad hunted down a local hangout to have dinner. We walked out of the touristy area into a residential neighborhood and found a restaurant that looked like someone's house. We had snapper caught that day, deep-fried whole and brought to the table on a beautiful platter with radishes, green onions, different salsas and tortillas. We pulled the strips off the fish and made them into tacos. It left such a lasting impression on me that I recreated the recipe." Here, classic margaritas, Lea de Wit's hand-blown glass sculpture and our Passionflower linens add fiesta-style fun.

crispy whole bass tacos

with avocado tomatillo salsa,
salsa quemada, cumin-lime
vinaigrette, coleslaw and beans

serves 4 to 6

AVOCADO TOMATILLO SALSA

½ pound tomatillos, cut in fourths
1 jalapeño, cut in fourths and seeded
1 clove garlic
½ bunch cilantro
½ cup chicken stock, room temperature
1 avocado
1 lemon, juiced
¾ teaspoon salt
Pinch black pepper

SALSA QUEMADA

5 Roma tomatoes, cut in half
7 tomatillos
13 serranos
½ jalapeño
6 cloves garlic
Pinch oregano
1 cup water, as needed
Salt and freshly ground black pepper, to taste

CUMIN-LIME VINAIGRETTE

½ clove garlic, diced and rinsed
½ shallot, diced and rinsed
½ cup orange juice
½ lime, juiced
1 tablespoon honey
½ tablespoon cumin seeds, toasted and ground
½ tablespoon chili powder
½ cup canola oil
6 bunches green onion, cleaned and blanched
Salt and freshly ground black pepper, to taste ▶

simon dolinky, kelvin

As a child, Simon Dolinky played sous chef for his mom, but before long, he progressed to cooking and baking on his own. A curious traveler, Simon found that experiencing different cultures provided an open-ended source for discovering new techniques and styles. He moved to San Diego specifically for the thriving organic small-farm scene. "Southern California has got to be one of the easiest places to be a locavore and certainly one of the most delicious!" Simon raves. "On a day-to-day basis, we can shop local, use all parts of the meat, fish or vegetables we purchase, spend less money on packaging and, in general, make decisions that help ensure a successful future not only in this business but in our lives."

COLESLAW

1/2 head red cabbage, sliced thin
1/2 head green cabbage, sliced thin
1/2 red onion, sliced thin

BEANS

4 cups dry pinto beans, picked over
4 heads garlic
2 oranges, zested
1 lemon, zested
1 leek
1 carrot
1 stalk celery
1 white onion
8 star anise
4 sprigs thyme
6 bay leaves
40 black peppercorns
12 cups water
Salt, to taste

SEABASS

1 (1 1/2- to 2-pound) whole bass, scaled and gutted
Salt and freshly ground black pepper, to taste
2 cups all-purpose flour
3 tablespoons cornstarch

FINISHING TOUCHES

Warm fresh tortillas

BEGIN the avocado tomatillo salsa by puréeing the tomatillos, jalapeño, garlic, cilantro, and stock in a blender until smooth. Add avocado and blend for 1 minute. Finish salsa with lemon juice and season with salt and freshly ground black pepper, to taste.

PREHEAT oven to 400ºF.

PREPARE the salsa quemada by lightly oiling and seasoning the tomatoes, tomatillos, serranos, and jalapeño and roast them until slightly charred. Purée roasted ingredients, garlic, oregano, and water in a blender until smooth. Season with salt and freshly ground black pepper, to taste.

MAKE the cumin-lime vinaigrette by puréeing the garlic, shallot, citrus juices, honey, and spices in a blender. Add oil in a slow steady stream and blend in blanched green onions to finish. Season with salt and freshly ground black pepper, to taste.

COMBINE all the coleslaw ingredients with cumin-lime vinaigrette and let sit at least 1 hour.

PREPARE the beans by tying the seasonings and vegetables in a large cheesecloth sachet. Place the sachet and beans in a stockpot with the water. Cover the pot with a lid halfway and gently simmer until the beans are tender, about 45 to 60 minutes. Once the beans are done, discard the cooked vegetables and spices. Remove the pot from the heat and drain off most of the cooking liquid, but leave enough to cover the beans. Salt the beans and let them soak up some of the salty cooking liquid until ready to serve.

MAKE 3 or 4 long diagonal cuts in the flesh of the bass and rub with salt and a little pepper. Combine flour and cornstarch, dredge fish inside and out, and carefully deep fry until golden brown and crispy. Drain on paper towels.

PLACE the whole bass on a large platter covered with a bed of coleslaw. Surround with bowls of beans, salsas and a pile of your favorite warm fresh tortillas.

lea de wit, lucky stripe studios

When she was just a teenager, a bone tumor in her spine propelled Lea de Wit to follow her passion. "I learned that life is too short not to pursue what you love. I have worked with various art forms my whole career, but when I started working with hot glass, I was hooked." Lea thrives on the challenges that glasswork presents. "Working with a medium that can be molten in one state and breakable in another state is an adventure," she explains. "The fine line between pliable and fragile makes glassblowing that much more challenging and intriguing. It allows for an endless number of options to sculpt and transform the molten material into interesting shapes." Her work for *Living Coastal* is pure ocean. "Each piece features a tonal range quintessential of water," Lea says. "I have manipulated the color design to create depth and motion. Additionally, I worked with a shape that mimics water droplets. Working in multiples, I hint at the sheer volume and vastness of the ocean." The resulting sculpture, even more magical when illuminated, spreads dappled light across the table and brings drama to the overall experience of the meal.

breezy beachside picnic

Is there any better way to feast *alfresco* style than by taking in sun and surf at a breezy seaside picnic? Add a level of eco-chic sophistication to the outing with reusable utensils, napkins and an assortment of delectable gourmet treats. The Sea Urchin Crostini from Sea Rocket Bistro Chef Tommy Fraioli is the perfect portable epicurean delight. He says, "I see it as an interesting seafood twist on my favorite picnic sandwich: salami, cheese and bread." Donna Butnik's lively jellyfish tablecloth paired with our Jellyfish napkins completes a marine scene that will surely whet your appetite!

sea urchin crostini

with roe-herb butter, jalapeño jam and lavender salt

serves 4

Chef's Notes: The crostini pairs nicely with Rough Draft Brewing Company's Freudian Sip beer.

ROE-HERB BUTTER
2 to 3 pieces urchin roe
$1/2$ pound (2 sticks) unsalted butter, softened
2 teaspoons mixed fresh herbs (parsley, chives, and thyme), minced

JALAPEÑO JAM
1 cup jalapeño, seeded and diced
$1/4$ cup granulated sugar
$1/2$ cup water
Salt, to taste

LAVENDER SALT
$1/2$ cup sea salt
1 tablespoon dried lavender

FINISHING TOUCHES
1 loaf ciabatta
4 pieces urchin roe

BLEND urchin roe in food processor until smooth. Add butter and herbs. Cover tightly in plastic wrap and refrigerate roe-herb butter until needed.
COMBINE jalapeño, sugar, water, and salt in a small saucepot and cook on medium heat until thick enough to coat the back of a spoon. Set aside until needed.
PLACE the sea salt and dried lavender in a coffee grinder and pulse until smooth.
SLICE bread to desired thickness and toast or grill. Spread on butter, add a piece of roe, and top with jam and a pinch of lavender salt.

tommy fraioli, sea rocket bistro

Tommy grew up in a Greek/Italian family in which most members cooked. "I was always in the kitchen watching my dad and grandparents make meals and trying to lend a hand," Tommy remembers. "Over the years, learning new things and working with great chefs has kept me committed." Tommy works with his established network of local farmers and fishermen to find unique ingredients that resonate with his customers. "The San Diego coastal region is great for sustainable food practices," he explains, "because we have access to a large variety of fresh local ingredients to choose from, including many varieties of fish, sea urchin and wonderful produce. San Diego has pretty much anything you might want to make a creative menu!"

living coastal

peter halmay

Back in the early seventies, Peter Halmay left his job as an engineer, bought a used lobster boat and began diving for sea urchin. He was as passionate about the ocean's health then as he is now. Suited up in well-worn scuba gear, Peter spends long hours underwater plucking the spiny creatures off rocks with a tool called a rake. He tends the kelp beds/sea urchin gardens to help maintain a balanced marine ecosystem. On land, he devotes his energy to working with other fishermen, environmental groups, scientists, students and chefs to keep the waters off Southern California a vital habitat for the native sea life and the local fishing community. As president of the San Diego Fishermen's Working Group, he is a tireless promoter of local, sustainable seafood. The fishermen of this group harvest an amazing 86 different species of local fish, including sablefish, sea bass and thornyhead. Peter advocates the centuries-old Sicilian idea of *cucina povera* (literally meaning "poor kitchen") — use whatever is available to prepare great food. With seafood, this means eating "from the top of the food chain down" instead of consuming only the top two or three predators. He hopes to see this practice supported by the Slow Food movement, restaurants and chefs who can spearhead dining trends by creating recipes that use lesser-known varieties of fish.

artist profile
donna butnik

Influenced by nature, dreams and proximity to the ocean, Donna Butnik developed a signature technique that has gained a local following. She uses drip enamel house paints that are rolled out layer by layer, slowly revealing a finished composition. "My best creations are when the painting paints itself," Donna says. "I just stand out of the way and let the drips turn into a visual melody." To achieve her distinctive style, she employs radiant colors to portray mythic, ethereal forms such as mermaids, sea creatures and — in this piece — an intensely saturated jellyfish.

cockleshells & birthday bells

A sunny beach theme promises to make your child's next birthday party an enchanting one. From cockleshells to crusty crustaceans, there's no limit on sea creatures to spark a child's imagination. Our table is a jovial jumble of aqua and blue, set with Kathleen McCord's fanciful aquatic plates, our Happy Crab napkins, shell-adorned recycled mason-jar glasses and a scrumptious birthday cake from Millie's Gelato. Terra American Bistro Chef Jeff Rossman cooks up a kid's favorite with a fun, modern twist: Mac and Cheese with Tuna Lollipops.

mac and cheese
with tuna lollipops

serves 4 to 6

3 cups whole milk
4 tablespoons unsalted butter
¼ cup all-purpose flour
10 ounces shredded cheese (use your favorite)
½ tablespoon kosher salt
1 teaspoon freshly ground black pepper
1 pound mini penne pasta, cooked *al dente*
2 to 3 strips cooked bacon, cut into 1-inch pieces
5 ounces raw broccoli florets, cut into small pieces
1 cup fresh corn, shaved off the cob
1 cup panko bread crumbs
1 tablespoon asiago or parmesan cheese
1½ pounds fresh ahi tuna, diced into 1-inch cubes
3 tablespoons olive oil
Salt and freshly ground black pepper, to taste

PREHEAT oven to 350°F.
HEAT milk in a saucepot over medium heat. In another saucepot, melt butter and whisk in flour. Cook on low heat for about 1 minute to "cook out" the flour. Add roux to hot milk and whisk continuously until fully combined. Lower heat to medium low and let thicken.
WHISK cheese into sauce until melted. Season with salt and pepper. Remove from heat.
COMBINE pasta, cheese sauce, bacon, broccoli, and corn in a bowl. Transfer to a 10x13-inch casserole dish or mini cast-iron skillets coated with nonstick spray.
MIX bread crumbs with asiago cheese and sprinkle evenly over the top. Bake uncovered for about 30 to 35 minutes.
PREHEAT a grill or a grillpan over high heat.
TOSS tuna in olive oil and sprinkle with salt and pepper. Skewer the pieces and grill for about 30 seconds per side, until just firm. Allow to cool.
POKE skewers into mac and cheese and serve.

jeff rossman, terra american bistro

Jeff grew up working in his family restaurant and developed a knack for cooking. Today, he loves to make people happy with simple, flavorful food. In keeping with the traditions of modern California cuisine, Jeff adapts his menus to the rhythm of the seasons by using locally grown food to create contemporary culinary twists. "Good ingredients are the cornerstone of good cooking," Jeff says. "But to be a great cook, you must trust your senses, especially your taste buds, and let the cooking come from within. Using all of your senses is the key to producing a flavorful dish: watch, listen, smell, touch and taste." Southern California's Mediterranean climate and unique topography enable farmers to grow many types of produce year round. However, the term *locally grown* can be misleading because some grocery store chains refer to *local* as anything that comes from California. Jeff advises, "Buy produce that comes from within 25 miles of your county line. This way you know you're not only supporting local or regional farmers, but you're also getting food that hasn't been sitting in a truck forever and has used a minimal amount of fossil fuel and other energy to reach you."

susan sbicca, millie's gelato

Award-winning chef Susan Sbicca became vegan in 2010 and saw a need for a good, healthy dessert that satisfied her newfound dietary restrictions. Incorporating her passion for preparing quality food to share with family and friends, she created a line of all natural, dairy-free, gluten-free incredibly delicious gelato. Susan named her line after her mother, Millie, who "always had something sweet going." She draws inspiration for new flavors from the holidays and traditions that come with each season. What is the secret to her success? "Using the best local ingredients and lots of love."

kathleen mccord

A master at drawing animated whimsical characters, Kathleen captures the hearts and minds of both children and adults. Her extensive research into marine life culminated in two books she illustrated for the Monterey Bay Aquarium. Accomplished in portraying the bubbly, magical world of the ocean, Kathleen expertly reproduces the quintessence of sea creatures in their environment. She used watercolor and gouache paints to create this aquatic fantasy for her colorful under-the-sea plate. "The art goes along the bottom and flows up the sides to frame the goodies that will be joyfully eaten on the plate," Kathleen explains. "My hope is that the art will enhance the children's party experience and make for an all-around fun day."

date night

There's nothing like an intimate candlelit dinner to relax and connect with the one you love. An ambrosial Asian-fusion supper can lead to romance. Create atmosphere by setting the table Japanese style, complete with hot towels, bamboo mats and chopstick rests. Matthew Antichevich's *Vertical Wave* sculpture and our Wave runner help to complete the surf-inspired scene. Partake of Zenbu Chef Tim Johnson's sensual Oysters with Uni and Lobster Ceviche while you fill each other's sake cups, raise them and customarily toast *Kanpai*!

oysters
with uni and lobster ceviche

serves 1

Chef's Notes: Invest in a good oyster knife with a narrow blade. When you begin to pry the oyster open, always twist the blade to pop it open. By forcing it straight in, you may damage the meat. The goal is to keep the oyster whole.

OYSTERS AND UNI
6 small oysters, shucked
Crushed ice
1 live sea urchin (uni), roe cleaned and divided into 6 pieces
6 thin round slices jalapeño
6 dashes ponzu sauce

CEVICHE
1 steamed Pacific spiny lobster, split in half, cleaned, meat removed
2 tablespoons salsa fresca
1/2 avocado, cubed
1 lime, juiced
Salt and freshly ground black pepper, to taste

FINISHING TOUCHES
Roe (I prefer baked spot prawn roe or masago or tobiko)
Lemon wedges
Microgreens
Tortilla chips

LAY oysters on a bed of crushed ice. Place a small piece of uni and a slice of jalapeño on each oyster. Garnish with baked spot prawn roe, a dash of ponzu sauce, and lemon wedges. **CUT** lobster meat in 1/2-inch pieces. In a bowl, mix lobster, salsa fresca, avocado, lime juice, and salt and freshly ground black pepper, to taste. Marinate refrigerated for 30 minutes. The lobster shell makes a great dish to hold the ceviche. **SERVE** oysters with a dish of the ceviche garnished with microgreens, a lemon wedge, and your favorite tortilla chips.

tim johnson, zenbu

Tim Johnson grew up watching his Japanese grandmother and mother prepare exceptional dishes that have always remained his favorite cuisine. Now at Zenbu, Tim delights in developing unique Asian dishes with a modern flair. "I get to meet so many great people, make guests smile and see that instant appreciation of all of my hard work." Owner Matt Rimel's eco-friendly seafood company, Ocean Giant, supplies his restaurants with seasonal, local and exotic fish daily. Prehistoric looking rockfish, spiky sea urchin and succulent California spiny lobster are notables on a menu bursting with fresh ocean bounty. Since its inception, Zenbu established a following for the delicacy of live uni scooped fresh from the restaurants' on-site tanks, cracked open and delivered to the table in all its creamy, oozy ocean gloriousness. "Let the flavors of what you are working with come out on their own," Chef Tim says. "You want to highlight them, not mask them with too many additions. Go out and find some local seafood to cook and eat raw. Keep it simple but experiment. Enjoy!"

whole foods market encinitas

This full-service seafood department preps all seafood for free: they'll fillet for you, season or marinate your favorite fish and even shuck your fresh oysters. *Made right here* specialties include honey chipotle crab cakes, wild salmon jalapeño burgers and the signature build-your-own-poke bowl, where customers can choose from ahi or salmon poke, house-made sauces, seaweed salad, Himalayan sea salt and sesame seeds over rice. All wild-caught fish is either certified sustainable by the Marine Stewardship Council or displayed with color-coded ratings developed by the Blue Ocean Institute and the Monterey Bay Aquarium. The market uses strict standards for aquaculture to make sure that farming practices do not cause water pollution or other damage to the environment. They prohibit the use of antibiotics, added growth hormones and poultry by-products in feed; additionally, they do not sell genetically modified seafood or allow added preservatives like sulfites and phosphates.

artist profile
matthew antichevich

Matthew's art is all about surfing and the ocean. He created the world famous 16-foot bronze statue of a surfer in Cardiff-by-the-Sea called *Magic Carpet Ride*. On a much smaller scale, *Vertical Drop* (shown in the tabletop spread) is no less striking. "My sculpture is bronze, a very ancient medium that withstands the test of time," Matthew explains. "The piece reveals a surfer taking the big drop. This act continues to challenge and break new barriers. Anyone who's made the drop knows the feeling, regardless of how big the wave was." To achieve his characteristic style, Matthew works mostly in wax. "I create numerous waxes used as waves with specific textures and swirls to imitate the ocean. Then I shape the wave or spray in a standing position. Finally I shape the character and movement to go with the flow. These works are one of kind."

chill'n & grill'n

A backyard barbecue is a great way to kick back, relax and have fun. Thanks to the mild climate, San Diegans enjoy entertaining outdoors nearly all year round. And with the cornucopia of local fresh seafood available, why not ditch the usual burger/dog option for a more adventurous catch of the day? Chef Mario Moser of the Flying Pig Pub & Kitchen suggests adding a Mediterranean twist to the classic American cookout by serving up Char-Grilled Octopus Salad. The dish is paired with Ballast Point's super-refreshing Pale Ale. Mark Patterson's captivating octopus mosaic table coordinates with our nautical pillows and Blue Wave napkins.

living coastal 83

char-grilled octopus salad

with farro, oven-roasted tomatoes and arugula

serves 4 to 6

Chef's Notes: Have your fishmonger remove the ink sacs from the octopuses.

FARRO
2 tablespoons extra virgin olive oil
1 cup farro
3 cups water
Pinch salt

ROASTED TOMATOES
16 to 18 cherry tomatoes
1 to 2 tablespoons olive oil
3 sprigs fresh thyme
Salt, to taste

POACHING LIQUID
2 Roma tomatoes, roughly chopped
5 cloves garlic
1 cup shallot, sliced
1 tablespoon red pepper flakes
1 lemon, cut in half
1 to 2 tablespoons olive oil
1 gallon water
3 to 4 pounds fresh whole octopus, ink sacs removed

MARINADE
6 tablespoons extra virgin olive oil
1 lemon, zested
1 lime, zested
1 tablespoon smoked paprika
1 tablespoon red pepper flakes
½ cup parsley, chopped ▶

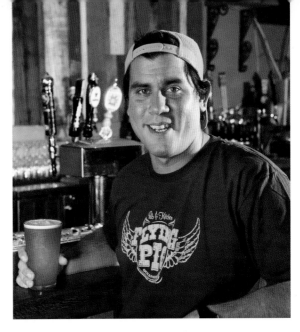

mario moser, flying pig pub & kitchen

Mario's love of good food and drink makes him a natural in the kitchen. He enjoys building flavors, creating, troubleshooting and "the irreverent and somewhat sophisticated culture innate to the industry." His approach to cooking specifically emphasizes farm-to-table cuisine. "Sustainable local foods avoid damaging the environment while at the same time support the local farmers, fishermen and purveyors who make the whole movement possible," Mario explains. "This is a very important trend for an area like San Diego where we have abundant farmers markets and a substantial fishing industry." Mario's octopus salad represents his rustic ingredient-driven style. "I only use octopus when I can get the fresh local stuff," he says. Octopus is a great ingredient, one of my favorites. I find it to be underrated. If done right, which usually means the simplest way possible, it always turns out tasty."

DRESSING
½ tablespoon Dijon mustard
1 tablespoon garlic, minced
½ cup champagne vinegar
1½ cups extra virgin olive oil
Salt, to taste

FINISHING TOUCHES
Fresh arugula

PREHEAT oven to 450°F.

HEAT olive oil in a small stockpot on medium heat. Add farro and toast lightly until golden brown and aromatic. Add water and bring to a boil. Turn the heat down to a simmer, add salt and cover until farro is tender. Drain and set aside.

TOSS cherry tomatoes in olive oil to coat and add sprigs of thyme and salt. Spread in one layer on a sheet pan and roast in the oven until skins split. Set aside.

SAUTÉ Roma tomatoes, garlic, shallot, red pepper flakes, and lemon in olive oil in a stockpot on high heat. Add water and bring to a boil. Turn the heat down to a simmer and add the octopuses. Simmer on low until tender, about 1 hour depending on the sizes of octopuses. Drain and cool. (You can save the cooking liquid and use it to poach fish again.)

CUT off octopus heads at the base and then in half the long way to remove the insides. Reserve skin and tissue and cut into strips. Slice the legs on a bias into pieces about ½ inch thick, leaving the ends intact.

PUT octopuses in a large bowl. Add olive oil, lemon and lime zests, smoked paprika, red pepper flakes, and parsley. Toss to coat octopuses thoroughly and marinate for a minimum of 30 minutes.

HEAT a grill to high. Grill octopuses until charred.

WHISK together mustard, garlic, and vinegar, and slowly drizzle olive oil in a constant stream to emulsify. Finish with salt.

PLACE the farro, octopus salad and roasted tomatoes on individual plates, drizzle with dressing, garnish with arugula, and serve.

ballast point brewing & spirits

Founded by San Diego native Jack White and named after a historic peninsula in Point Loma near his childhood home, Ballast Point Brewing & Spirits is truly one of San Diego's homegrown success stories. Even the fish-centric names of Ballast Point's beers reinforce the company's connection to its marine-influenced home. Recognized for its impressive array of beers and beer styles, the brewery is perhaps best known for its crisp, balanced and intensely flavored ales, including their award-winning and highly coveted Sculpin IPA. Ballast Point's master brewers, Yuseff Cherney and Colby Chandler, create craft beers and spirits that often pay homage to the dizzying array of local ingredients available in the region. Colby, for example, makes a San Diego Farmhouse Ale that is flavored with manzanita berries, pine nuts, honey and white sage.

artist profile mark patterson

Mark Patterson (pictured above) and his friend Bob Nichols clandestinely installed Mark's *Save the Ocean* mosaic (also known as *Surfing Madonna*) under the train tracks in Encinitas. Almost immediately, the controversial work thrust Mark into the international spotlight. The mosaic was intended as a gift to the community to encourage environmental stewardship. Mark's commitment to ocean preservation is playfully reflected in his *Wily Octopus Table* featured in this spread. "The octopus is an incredibly intelligent being and is extremely sensitive to toxic runoff from shore as well as tanker flushing at sea." Mark insists that this local delicacy deserves to be recognized for its beauty and intelligence. And he hopes "readers become aware that they can make a difference by not dumping oil or other toxic chemicals down the storm drains. Long term, this impacts everyone, not just sea creatures." The juxtaposition of the culinary and visual arts as a way to create a joyous communal experience is important to Mark. He hopes that his octopus table will simultaneously delight and entertain the viewer: "Although she sits in her kelp bed looking serene, she is also sneaking her tentacles under the table top looking for goodies. She's a little mischievous — maybe like some of your dinner guests!"

haunting halloween

Flesh-eating zombie alert! This is a night to delve into the dark side and celebrate with a phantasmagorical affair, coastal style. The decor is black; the mood spooky, heightened with murky cobwebs, bleeding candles and oh-so-creepy-crawly edibles. Waypoint Public Chef Amanda Baumgarten concocted a sinister-looking whole baked fish for the occasion — which looks eerie but tastes divine. For libation, blood-dripping Venom Bite cocktails are the drink of choice. Artists Julie Ann Stricklin and Danny Salzhandler teamed up to create an over-the-top pirate gothic candelabra complete with kraken gong. Their fabulous creation is set off by our scary octopus tentacle rings that coil around our velvety purple Starfish napkins.

whole baked fish

serves 2

Chef's Notes: When you purchase your fish, ask your fishmonger to scale it and remove the gills and guts.

FISH
1 (2-pound) whole snapper or any similar size fish, gutted and scaled
Kosher salt and freshly ground black pepper, to taste
4 ($\frac{1}{8}$-inch) lemon slices
1 clove fresh garlic, smashed
2 sprigs fresh oregano
1 to 2 tablespoons olive oil

FINISHING TOUCHES
Arugula
Orange sections
Lemon slices
Pine nuts, toasted
1 tablespoon capers
1 tablespoon extra virgin olive oil
$\frac{1}{4}$ lemon, juiced

FIRE up your wood-burning oven or preheat a conventional oven to 375°F.
SEASON the fish inside and out with salt and pepper. Stuff the cavity with lemon slices, garlic, and oregano.
GREASE a large piece of parchment paper with olive oil. Lay the fish down on the paper and roll the paper up around the fish. Tie both ends with some butcher's twine, and place the fish on a sheet tray, then into the oven for 15 to 20 minutes. Test the doneness by sticking a knife through the parchment and into the fish. If it is hot to the touch, your fish is done.
PLACE the cooked fish on a large serving platter. Unwrap the parchment and garnish the platter with arugula, orange sections, lemon slices, toasted pine nuts, and capers. Drizzle with extra virgin olive oil and lemon juice.

amanda baumgarten, waypoint public

Raised in a family that dined out frequently, Amanda developed an appreciation of restaurants at a young age. "I loved the process of going out to dinner," Amanda remembers. When she grew older, Amanda "woke up one day and decided to be a chef." That decision led her to an internship at L'Orangerie in Los Angeles for six months. At the end of her training, she was hooked! "I love the camaraderie of the kitchen and how you get out of the profession directly what you put in," Amanda says. "I enjoy the adrenalin rush and being busy." After L'Orangerie, she attended Le Cordon Bleu in London, ultimately appearing on Bravo's hit reality show *Top Chef*. Amanda focuses on farm-driven produce and local seafood. "I like to let the seafood be the star of the show and not mess with it too much," she explains. "That's pretty much my philosophy for all ingredients." Her whole baked fish is an excellent example. "I like it because it's simple. The flavor is the fish roasted in a wood-burning oven. The lemon slices caramelize on top and the sauce is uncomplicated — just orange, lemon, capers and olive oil."

venom vodka

Veteran firemen Kim Blaylock and Mark Miceli came up with the idea for Venom Vodka while hanging out on the pristine Colorado River. They named their product for the venomous desert wildlife that surrounded them in the area. Kim proudly explains, "Venom was the 2012 Gold Medal winner in taste at the Micro Liquor Spirit Awards. It is a handcrafted spirit made in small batches using a unique filtration system. The vodka is made with pure cascade mountain spring water and all natural grain. It is distilled five times and filtered six times through crushed lava rock, onyx and diamonds, which gives it a unique ultra-smooth taste." Because the spirit has been well received and supported by a network of restaurants and markets, Venom has established strong ties with the local business community. And the company believes in giving back: a portion of all proceeds from bottle sales supports firefighter charities.

venom bite cocktail

created by david eliason, venom vodka mixologist

serves 1

2 ounces Venom Ultra-Premium Vodka
2 ounces White Godiva Chocolate Liqueur
1 ounce Crème de Cacao
$\frac{1}{2}$ ounce Chambord

HALLOWEEN TOUCHES
Black sugar
Cherry syrup
Plastic spider

COMBINE all ingredients in a shaker and shake vigorously before straining into a martini glass. For fun, rim the glass with black sugar, drip some cherry syrup into the drink to look like blood, and float a plastic spider on top or attach it to the stem.

artists profile julie ann stricklin and danny salzhandler

Longtime friends Julie Ann Stricklin and Danny Salzhandler collaborated on the spirited nautical-themed creation featured for Halloween. "The centerpiece was designed as a vampire/gothic/steam punk/pirate candelabra with an evil kraken gong for a formal dinner," Julie Ann explains. To construct their piece, they selected repurposed and found objects that they salvaged outside of Danny's welding studio. Machine equipment parts were transformed into a solid industrial base, and a central glowing gem made out of beach glass provides ghostly ambiance. Small elements, such as skeleton keys and spider webs, are placed throughout the piece to spark flights of fancy. "The centerpiece is the muse for storytelling and imagination," Julie Ann adds. "Even while creating the piece, Danny and I imagined it on a pirate's table and a monstrous captain screaming while he hit the gong to demand attention."

weekend brunch

Hosting a brunch is an easy, flexible way to entertain. Set out freshly brewed coffee, pitchers of juice, mugs and glasses for guests to help themselves. Spice things up with Mimosas, Bloody Marys or Bellinis. Fill out the spread with some seasonal fruit and fresh-baked Ginger Pear Scones from Claire's on Cedros. For a mouthwatering main, prepare Salmon Benedict, one of the most popular brunch dishes at Chef Matt Gordon's Solace & The Moonlight Lounge. "It's definitely a different take on benedicts," Matt explains. "We use our really yummy homemade biscuits made out of two kinds of flour, two kinds of cheese, lots of butter and chives. We wilt a little bit of organic spinach on the biscuits and add the poached eggs. Then we make a delectable ancho chili hollandaise for the top using ground whole anchos, chipotle powder, smoked paprika, cayenne and lemon. It gives it a really nice smoky, mildly spicy finish." Copper fish from sculptor Charles Bronson add a touch of whimsy to the table alongside our Fish napkins.

sockeye salmon benedict

on cheese and chive biscuits with ancho chili hollandaise

serves 6

Chef's Notes: You can put the poached eggs in ice water and rewarm them gently if you want to make them an hour or two ahead of time.

BISCUITS
3 cups pastry flour
3 cups all-purpose flour
1¹/₂ tablespoons baking powder
2 teaspoons kosher salt
3 sticks unsalted butter
3 cups white cheddar cheese, shredded
1¹/₂ cups fontina cheese, grated
¹/₄ cup fresh chives, minced
2¹/₂ to 3 cups buttermilk
Egg whites, optional

ANCHO CHILI HOLLANDAISE
6 egg yolks
1 teaspoon cold water
1 cup clarified butter, heated but not too hot
1 teaspoon lemon juice
1 teaspoon ancho chili powder
¹/₂ teaspoon chipotle powder
¹/₂ teaspoon smoked paprika
¹/₄ teaspoon cayenne pepper
Salt and freshly ground black pepper, to taste

EGGS
2 quarts water
¹/₄ cup white wine vinegar
12 organic local eggs

SOCKEYE SALMON
Salt and freshly ground black pepper, to taste
3 pounds wild salmon, cleaned and trimmed into
    3-ounce pieces (2 medallions per person)
Vegetable oil, for searing

SPINACH
Fresh organic spinach
Butter
Salt and freshly ground black pepper, to taste

FINISHING TOUCHES
Fresh chives and parsley, chopped

PREHEAT oven to 400ºF (use convection if available). SIFT together biscuit flours, baking powder, and salt. Add butter, cheeses, and chives, and mix with a pastry knife or paddle attachment of a mixer to incorporate the butter. Leave some small chunks of butter; this will make the biscuit flaky. Add buttermilk and slowly fold together. Do not overmix the dough. On a lightly floured work surface, knead 2 or 3 times only. Flatten dough to about ¾ inch thickness and cut in desired shape. Brush top with egg whites (optional) and bake for 12 to 14 minutes. If you are not using a convection oven, it will probably take a bit longer. When biscuits are golden brown, crack one open to make sure it is cooked inside. If not, lower heat to 250ºF and check again in a couple of minutes.

WHISK yolks and water in a steel bowl over a double boiler until slightly thickened (about 120ºF). Remove from heat and slowly whisk in clarified butter a little at a time until incorporated. Add remaining ingredients and hold the hollandaise sauce in a warm waterbath until ready to serve.

BRING a pot of water to a boil, add vinegar, and reduce heat to a simmer. Take a large ladle and stir the water vigorously to form a whirlpool. Quickly crack an egg into the ladle and gently lower it into the whirlpool. Repeat with as many eggs you can do in about 20 seconds (6 per pot is good). Simmer for 3 minutes, remove with a slotted spoon, and serve immediately or place in a bowl of warm water if you are holding them only for a few minutes.

SEASON salmon pieces. Heat a skillet on high until almost smoking. Coat the bottom of the pan with oil, and when it starts to shimmer, carefully place a piece of salmon in the pan; it should sizzle. Quickly sear on each side. Keep medium rare if possible. This takes only about 2 minutes. Repeat with remaining salmon pieces. SAUTÉ a little organic baby spinach in a touch of butter with a pinch of salt and pepper to slightly wilt.

SPLIT each biscuit in half and toast in the oven or in a pan. On each biscuit half, place two or three spinach leaves, one salmon medallion, and a poached egg. Finish with a ladle of hollandaise. Garnish with fresh herbs.

matt gordon,
solace & the moonlight lounge

Matt Gordon originally aspired to become a musician. He now heads up three restaurants: Urban Solace, Solace & the Moonlight Lounge and Sea & Smoke. Matt endeavors to select quality purveyors and to deliver great ingredients to his patrons. "First and foremost, we're a restaurant," Matt explains, "so our main goal is to provide great food and great service. We don't compromise on what we purchase: we know who raises the cattle, where all of our chicken comes from and the fisherman who catches our salmon." Matt purchases sockeye salmon from Bristol Bay Salmon Company, one of the premier fisheries in the world. "As everybody's aware, there's a very questionable future in wild fish; one of the reasons we like this product so much is it's extremely well-managed. It's easy to oversee how the fish swim and spawn and to estimate how many salmon survive before fishing is allowed to happen. Bristol Bay's boat has the highest rating certification for how they treat fish. The salmon are really pristine because they are caught and kept only a certain amount of time in saltwater holds before being filleted and flash-frozen within hours of harvest."

ginger pear scones

makes 8 scones

2¼ cups all-purpose or pastry flour
⅓ cup granulated sugar
1 tablespoon baking powder
⅔ cup crystalized ginger, finely chopped
1½ sticks (6 ounces) cold butter, cut into 1 inch cubes
1 ripe pear, cored, peeled, and diced
½ to ¾ cups heavy cream, plus extra for brushing tops
Crystal sugar, for decorating tops of scones

PREHEAT oven to 400°F.

PUT flour, sugar, baking powder, and crystalized ginger into the bowl of an electric mixer. Mix on low speed until well combined. While still on low, add butter piece by piece and continue beating until mixture has the consistency of fine meal. Remove bowl from mixer. Create a well in the center of the dough, and pour in the cream and diced pears. Using one hand, draw in the dry ingredients, mixing until just combined. If the mixture feels dry, add a little more cream.

TURN the dough out onto a lightly floured work surface and knead gently into a ball. Flatten the dough ball into a circle about ¾ inch thick. Cut into desired shapes. Place scones 1 inch apart on a parchment-lined sheet tray. Brush with extra cream and sprinkle with crystal sugar. Bake 12 to 16 minutes until lightly browned.

claire allison, claire's on cedros

At sixteen years old, Claire Allison worked as a dishwasher for a summer camp in the Sierra Nevada Mountains. A charismatic cook pulled her off the dishwashing line to help him bake bread. The cook's charm and ability to create wonderful food with meager resources sparked Claire's interest in "all things culinary." She went on to develop the famous Milton's Multigrain Bread recipe. Claire now runs Claire's on Cedros, and her basic philosophy is: "Start at the beginning with the best ingredients available whenever possible." Her popular LEED-certified restaurant in Solana Beach attests to her successful strategy. "We make most things from scratch because food tastes better, and you control what goes into the end product. The nice bonus is saving money on food costs." Claire's employs green practices to lessen its impact on the environment. Food ingredients are maximized, while green garbage, coffee grounds and egg crates are either repurposed or recycled. Claire's also provides delicious food such as their tasty Ginger Pear Scones. "My experience with most bakery scones is that they are dry," Claire explains. "With our scones, we use cream and butter to make them rich and moist. Pears are a natural when paired with ginger. In the summertime, we swap pears for equally delicious fresh peaches. The secret to a delicate crumb on a scone is to mix only until the dough comes together. Don't be tempted to overmix."

artist profile
charles bronson

Those who live close to the deep blue waters of the California coast are inevitably connected to the awe-inspiring force of the Pacific Ocean. Yet this awesome energy is often balanced by the calm, unhurried vibe of most beach environments. Copper artist Charles Bronson relishes this synergy where the ocean's strength meets the sun-drenched shores and open skies. This identification fuels his passion to sculpt wonderful, shimmering creations such as the *Going Coastal* fish sculpture we highlight here. He starts his pieces by visualizing them in his mind, so that he becomes a part of the concept in a "creative artistic fusion." Once the idea gels, he goes to his workbench to transform "Mother Nature's materials into art." Charles sees a duality between seafood and art. "Seafood, wine and art are perfect companions. Our coastal communities abound with chefs who bring culinary delights to our tables. We surround our experience with coastal decor, the ocean for background music and our senses as our guides."

home for the holidays

The holiday season is a scintillating time for coastal entertaining at its best; families gather to appreciate each other and the special memories that they create together. Set an elaborate table, prepare a resplendent meal and savor the good times in great company! Marine Room Chef Bernard Guillas crafts an indulgent and satisfying course for such a memorable occasion: Maine Diver Scallops and Baja Prawns. "This dish showcases a symphony of sustainable flavors encompassing both coasts," Bernard explains. Artfully plated on Mike Totah's exquisite handcrafted stoneware, the meal's aesthetic is further enhanced by Garry Cohen's hand-blown glassware and our festive shell-colored Seahorse linens.

maine diver scallops and baja prawns

with red quinoa and icewine-eggplant foam

serves 6

Chef's Notes: Start recipe two days in advance. You will also need a Thermo Whip cream maker for the foam (available at amazon.com and Williams-Sonoma).

PAIN D'ÉPICES CRISPS
1¹/₂ cups whole milk
1 cup dark brown sugar
1¹/₂ cups honey
1 orange, zested
2 lemons, zested
1 teaspoon ground star anise
1 teaspoon ground ginger
¹/₂ teaspoon ground cinnamon
¹/₂ teaspoon ground coriander
¹/₂ teaspoon ground cloves
¹/₄ teaspoon ground nutmeg
Pinch sea salt (I prefer Fleur de Sel)
4 cups all-purpose flour
2 large eggs
2 teaspoons baking soda
1 tablespoon water

HAZELNUT DUKKAH SPICE
¹/₄ cup hazelnuts, peeled
¹/₄ cup white sesame seeds
¹/₈ cup sliced almonds
2 tablespoons sunflower seeds, shelled
1 teaspoon coriander seeds
1 teaspoon cumin seeds
¹/₂ teaspoon fennel seeds
¹/₂ teaspoon sea salt
¹/₄ teaspoon freshly ground black pepper ▶

bernard guillas, the marine room

As a boy, Chef Bernard Guillas developed a passion for cooking by watching his grandmother make perfect, pristine crepes over a rudimentary wood fire stove in Brittany, France. He reminisces about her caring for the garden, orchard and animals. And he lovingly recalls wonderful family get-togethers. "Every Friday, Saturday and Sunday, the family would gather in the old farmhouse to celebrate life," Bernard recalls. There, he learned to appreciate flavor, the fragrance of an herb garden and the great honey that came from a huge tree in the corner of the garden. "Years later, I realized that the herbs were used to enhance the fragrance of my grandmother's cooking," Bernard says. "As a child, you keep those imprints lodged forever. Today's Slow Food movement is actually the mirror image of my childhood, but I have a better understanding of its importance."

⅛ teaspoon paprika
Pinch cayenne pepper

RED QUINOA
2 cups red quinoa
4 cups water
¼ cup red onion, chopped
½ cup fresh cilantro, chopped
½ cup fresh mint, chopped
½ cup fresh opal basil, chopped
⅓ cup extra virgin olive oil
¼ cup tangerine juice
1 ripe avocado, diced
Sea salt and freshly ground black pepper, to taste

SCALLOPS AND PRAWNS
12 (U-10) size Maine diver scallops
12 (U-10) Baja prawns, peeled, deveined, tail on
Salt and freshly ground black pepper
4 tablespoons extra virgin olive oil
2 tablespoons unsalted butter
4 tablespoons Dukkah spice

EGGPLANT FOAM
2 cups eggplant, peeled and diced
1 lemon, juiced and zested
1 teaspoon sea salt
2 tablespoons olive oil
1 clove garlic, smashed
2 tablespoons shallots, chopped
1 teaspoon thyme leaves
1 cup heavy cream
½ cup coconut milk
2 tablespoons icewine vinegar (I prefer Minus 8 brand)
1 teaspoon truffle oil
Sea salt and freshly ground white pepper, to taste

FINISHING TOUCHES
¼ cup celery sprouts (or other sprouts)
6 pain d'épices crisps
Kumquat confit, optional
6 pickled zucchini blossoms, optional

PREHEAT oven to 250°F.

HEAT milk, brown sugar, and honey in a saucepan. Add zests, spices, and salt and bring to a boil. Set aside to cool to room temperature. Sift flour into a bowl and make a well in the center. Add milk mixture and incorporate with a wooden spoon, gradually drawing in flour to make a smooth dough. Cover and refrigerate pain d'épices dough 8 hours or overnight.

WHISK eggs. Dissolve baking soda in water. Combine baking soda water into eggs and stir eggs into the dough. Butter and flour two loaf pans. Divide the batter evenly between the pans and allow to rest until the batter warms to room temperature. Bake approximately 90 minutes, or until a skewer inserted near the center comes out clean.

TRANSFER to a wire rack to cool. Wrap in plastic and freeze overnight. (The frozen loaves will be the consistency of banana bread but a little more moist.)

PREHEAT oven to 250°F.

CUT frozen loaves into ⅛-inch-thick slices with a serrated knife and transfer to a sheet tray. Bake for 45 minutes or until crisp. Cool on wire rack.

PREHEAT oven to 350°F.

PLACE hazelnuts, sesame seeds, almonds, and sunflower seeds for the Dukkah Spice in a single layer on a sheet tray. Roast in the oven for 10 minutes. Cool. Place coriander, cumin, and fennel seeds in a small skillet and toast over medium-low heat until fragrant. Place in food processor with nuts and remaining ingredients, and pulse until mixture is crumbly. Cool, and store in airtight container.

WASH quinoa under running water. Place in medium pan, add water, and bring to boil. Reduce heat to low. Cover, and simmer until liquid is absorbed, 10 to 15 minutes. Remove from heat. Fluff with a fork. Quinoa will be somewhat translucent. Transfer quinoa to sheet tray to cool quickly. Transfer quinoa to a bowl, and gently combine with remaining quinoa ingredients. Season with sea salt and freshly ground black pepper, to taste. Pack in a 2-ounce timbale for each serving.

PREHEAT oven to 375°F.

SEASON scallops and prawns with salt and pepper.

Add 2 tablespoons olive oil and 1 tablespoon butter to large cast-iron skillet. When butter is lightly browned and foamy, place scallops in skillet. Cook 1 minute on each side. Transfer to baking dish. Repeat process with prawns. Generously sprinkle Dukkah Spice on top of scallops and prawns. Bake 5 minutes or until slightly underdone.

TOSS eggplant, lemon juice, zest, and sea salt in a bowl. Let stand 5 minutes. Add oil to large saucepan over medium heat. Add eggplant, garlic, shallots, and thyme. Cook for 5 minutes without browning, stirring often. Add heavy cream and coconut milk, and bring to simmer. Reduce by half. Transfer mixture to blender, and purée until smooth. Strain through fine sieve. Whisk in icewine vinegar and truffle oil. Season with sea salt and white pepper to taste. Transfer to Thermo Whip cream maker and whip following manufacturer's instructions.

UNMOLD quinoa in center of a heated large deep plate. Arrange scallops and prawns beside quinoa. Dispense foam at the base of the scallops and prawns. Garnish with celery sprouts, pain d'épices crisps, kumquat confit and pickled zucchini, if desired. Repeat for remaining servings.

naturally to your door

Looking for a convenient way to stock up on local organic produce in the San Diego area? Naturally To Your Door is the perfect solution. Health food enthusiasts Vic and Marissa Curro started their company to provide easy access to farm-fresh fruits, vegetables, herbs and natural products from local San Diego farms delivered to your door.

artist profile
garry cohen,
glass ranch studio

Master craftsman Garry Cohen became interested in glassblowing in the early eighties when he started teaching at Palomar College. "There's no other surface like glass," he says. "The fluidity of the material when molten provides the ability to influence it using just your hands and simple tools." Guided by the substance's natural beauty, Garry characterizes his style as both colorful and whimsical. He came up with his easy-to-hold-and-store square glasses to offer items that can be used daily and are "unusual functional vessels out of the mainstream for useable dinnerware."

artist profile
mike totah, the wheel

Mike Totah and his coast-dwelling staff at The Wheel create stunning handmade ceramic dishes with an organic, free-flowing essence. Producing primarily for restaurants, Mike strives to marry the environs where his stoneware will be used with the food to be served on it. "For example, the setting of the Montage in Laguna Beach on the cliffs overlooking the ocean is pure drama," he says. "Our platters and bowls match that drama with seafoam glaze pooling into a forest-like background." Mike deliberately blends his art with qualities of its eventual owner. "Anyone can use a white plate," he explains. "But I find that the plate is the canvas for the chef. We want to present not only the best-tasting meal but also the most beautiful." Mike maintains that visually engaging dinnerware makes the entire dining experience infinitely more enjoyable. "It always surprises me how many people notice that the plates are handmade objects — full of life and character that just can't be faked."

wabisabi green™
modern home decor eco style

Wabisabi Green is artisanal quality, eco-friendly home decor and gifts featuring dazzling bold designs for green living. The modern collection of stylish decorative throw pillows and table linens are made of the best organic and sustainable materials sourced worldwide. Inspired by nature, these durable eco goods are created to bring art, color and comfort to your home. Designed, printed and fabricated in America.

wabisabigreen.com

resources

ARTISTS

Jolee Pink
Wabisabi Green:
Modern Home Decor Eco Style
wabisabi@cox.net
760.445.9225
wabisabigreen.com

Matthew Antichevich
Susan Hays Art Consultant
susanhaysartconsultant@gmail.com
760.473.2836

Karen Athens
Athens Design: Travel Destination
Paintings and Primitive Future
Sculptures
karenreal1@yahoo.com
be.net/karenathens

Charles Bronson
cbhome1@juno.com
760.630.0942
artist-charles-bronson.net

Donna Butnik
donna@artpaintings4decor.com
artpaintings4decor.com

Garry Cohen
Glass Ranch Studio
garrycohenstudio@gmail.com
760.745.7020
glassranchstudio.com

Lea de Wit
Lucky Stripe Studios
lea@luckystripe.com
760.310.7593
luckystripe.com

Elon Ebanks
Elon Ebanks Designs
deepart@cox.net
760.945.7441
sdvag.net

Stan Gafner
Studio95zero
sg@stangafner.com
760.586.0001
stangafner.com

Kathleen McCord
kathimccord@cox.net
619.850.2142

Britton Neubacher
Tend: Sustainable
Botanical Design
tending@tendliving.com
858.876.TEND (8363)
tendliving.com

Mark Patterson
Leucadia Creative Arts
mdpinsd@yahoo.com
760.473.6468
www.surfingmadonna.org

Danny Salzhandler
Biosculptures
salzhand@speakeasy.net
760.944.6027
biosculptures.com

James Stone
Stone and Glass: Glass Blowing
and Mixed Media Sculpture Studio
and Gallery
james@stoneandglass.com
858.485.7701
stoneandglass.com

Julie Ann Stricklin
Graphic Design/Illustration/Fine Art
info@julieannstricklin.com
julieannstricklin.com

Grace Swanson
Gourds By Grace
swanson121@cox.net
gourdsbygrace.com

Cheryl Tall
Cheryl Tall Art Studio
1114 North Coast Highway 101
Suite 2, Leucadia, CA 92024
cheryltall@earthlink.net
760.479.0399
cheryltall.com

Tara Teipel
Lemongrass: Center For Well-Being
910 Second Street
Encinitas, CA 92024
taranel@earthlink.net
760.633.1970
lemongrasscenter.com

Mike Totah
The Wheel: Handmade
Commercial Stoneware
thewheel88@sbcglobal.net
760.942.2351
thewheelstoneware.com

BUSINESSES

Ballast Point Brewing & Spirits
10051 Old Grove Road
San Diego, CA 92131
858.695.2739
ballastpoint.com

Bon Affair
444 South Cedros Avenue #175
Solana Beach, CA 92075
805.259.9327
bonaffair.com

Catalina Offshore
5202 Lovelock Street
San Diego, CA 92110
619.704.3639
catalinaop.com

Fallbrook Winery
554 Via Rancheros
Fallbrook, CA 92028
760.728.0156
fallbrookwinery.com

Peter Halmay
peterhalmay@gmail.com
619.957.7121
facebook.com/pages/San-
Diego-Fishermens-Working-
Group/100773763351039

La Jolla Beach & Tennis Club
2000 Spindrift Drive
La Jolla, CA 92037
888.828.0948
ljbtc.com

Millie's Gelato
info@milliesgelato.com
760.271.8641
milliesgelato.com

Naturally To Your Door
info@naturallytoyourdoor.com
858.946.6882
naturallytoyourdoor.com

Niche
119 Mozart Avenue
Cardiff-by-the-Sea, CA 92007
718.781.2877
niche-design.com

Sea Salt Candy Company
1910 Shadowridge Drive
Vista, CA 92081
760.727.5407
seasaltcandy.com

Smoke & Mirrors Cocktail Company
chris@smokeandmirrorscocktails.com
619.592.2042
smokeandmirrorscocktails.com

Stone Farms
9928 Protea Gardens Road
Escondido, CA 92026
951.226.4986
stonebrewing.com/farm

Venom Vodka
2770 Wilson Street
Carlsbad CA 92008
760.666.4976
venomvodka.com

Whole Foods Market
687 South Coast Highway 101
Encinitas, CA 92024
760.274.1580
wholefoodsmarket.com/stores/
encinitas

CHEFS/RESTAURANTS

Alchemy Cultural Fare & Cocktails
1503 30th Street
San Diego, CA 92102
619.255.0616
alchemysandiego.com

Andrew Spurgin
Bespoke Event Styling
& Menu Design
info@andrewspurgin.com
andrewspurgin.com

Chandler's
Hilton Carlsbad Oceanfront
Resort & Spa
1 Ponto Road
Carlsbad, CA 92011
855.683.5500
chandlerscarlsbad.com

Claire's on Cedros
246 North Cedros Avenue
Solana Beach, CA 92075
858.259.8597
clairesoncedros.com

The Fishery
5040 Cass Street
San Diego, CA 92109
858.272.9985
thefishery.com

Flying Pig Pub & Kitchen
626 South Tremont Street
Oceanside, CA 92054
760.453.2940
flyingpigpubkitchen.com

Kelvin
W San Diego Hotel
421 West B Street
San Diego, CA 92101
619.398.3082
kelvinrestaurant.com

The Marine Room
2000 Spindrift Drive
San Diego, CA 92037
858.459.7222
marineroom.com

MIHO Gastrotruck
info@MIHOgastrotruck.com
mihogastrotruck.com

Sea Rocket Bistro
3382 30th Street
San Diego, CA 92104
619.255.7049
searocketbistro.com

Sessions Public
4204 Voltaire Street
San Diego, CA 92107
619.756.7715
sessionspublic.com

**Solace & the
Moonlight Lounge**
25 East E Street
Encinitas, CA 92024
760.753.2433
eatatsolace.com

Starlite
3175 India Street
San Diego, CA 92103
619.358.9766
starlitesandiego.com

**Stone Brewing World
Bistro & Gardens —
Escondido**
1999 Citracado Parkway
Escondido, CA 92029
760.294.7866
stoneworldbistro.com

Terra American Bistro
7091 El Cajon Boulevard
San Diego, CA 92115
619.293.7088
terrasd.com

URBN Coal Fired Pizza
3885 University Avenue
San Diego, CA 92104
619.255.7300
urbnnorthpark.com

Waypoint Public
3794 30th Street
San Diego, CA 92104
amanda@waypointpublic.com
facebook.com/WaypointPublic

Zenbu
7660 Fay Avenue
San Diego, CA 92037
858.454.4540
zenburestaurants.com

recipe index